BREAK FREE TO PROSPER

FROM HARDSHIP TO SUCCESS

DESMOND RAWLINS

TABLE OF CONTENT

Page

CHAPTER ONE

INTRODUCTION

In the tapestry of life, each thread weaves a unique story: a tale of challenges, triumphs and the never-ending quest for prosperity. Life, in its countless forms, confronts us with obstacles that test our courage and often push us to the limits of our abilities. However, in the crucible of adversity lies the potential for transformation, to free ourselves from the chains that bind us and achieve the pinnacle of success.

Welcome to "Break Free to Prosper: From Hardship to Success." This book is not just a guide; is an invitation to embark on a profound journey of self-discovery, resilience and empowerment. It is a road map that navigates the winding paths of personal and professional growth, offering ideas and strategies not only for overcoming difficulties, but also for thriving in the face of adversity.

EMBRACE CHANGE

Change is the only constant in life and the ability to accept it is the first step to prosperity. On this journey, we will explore the power of transformation and how it can be harnessed to free yourself from the chains of self-doubt and limiting beliefs.

THE JOURNEY AHEAD

The path to success is strewn with pitfalls, but it is also strewn with opportunities for growth and fulfillment. Over the course of the chapters that follow, we'll delve deeper into the areas of mindset, resilience, financial empowerment, and the complex web of relationships that shape our lives.

So buckle up, open your mind to the possibilities, and let's embark on this transformative odyssey together. "Break Free to Prosper" is not just a book; It is a companion in your journey from difficulties to success. Let's turn the page and begin this stimulating adventure.

CHAPTER TWO

BREAK THE CHAINS

"Breaking chains" is a metaphorical expression that means liberation from bonds, limitations, or oppressive forces that hinder personal or collective progress. The metaphor is often used to describe the process of overcoming obstacles, breaking free from self-imposed limitations, or challenging social norms that limit one's potential.

In the context of personal development and empowerment, breaking chains can involve letting go of doubts, overcoming fears, challenging limiting beliefs, and adopting a mindset that promotes growth and growth. resilience. It's about freeing yourself from psychological or emotional barriers that could prevent you from reaching your full potential.

On a broader societal level, breaking chains can also refer to addressing systemic injustices, advocating for social change, and dismantling structures that oppress individuals or communities.

At its core, "breaking the chains" embodies the idea of emancipation, empowerment, and the quest for freedom, whether internal, such as freeing oneself from mental limitations, or external, involving efforts to question and change social norms or structures.

IDENTIFY LIMITING BELIEFS

In the complex tapestry of the human mind, beliefs weave the fabric of our reality. They shape our thoughts, influence our decisions and ultimately determine the course of our lives. However, not all beliefs move us forward; some act as insidious chains, limiting our potential and inhibiting our quest for prosperity. Identifying limiting beliefs is an essential step in the transformative journey from difficulties to success.

The nature of beliefs

Beliefs, conscious and subconscious, serve as lenses through which we perceive the world. These are the filters that shape our interpretations of events, influencing our emotions and behaviors. While empowering beliefs can propel us toward our goals, limiting beliefs have the opposite effect, acting as invisible barriers that hinder progress.

Conscious and subconscious beliefs

Conscious beliefs are those that we are aware of: beliefs that we can easily express and recognize. Subconscious beliefs, on the other hand, lurk beneath the surface and often influence our thoughts and actions without us being explicitly aware of them. It is in this area of subconscious beliefs where many limiting notions take root.

The impact of limiting beliefs

Limiting beliefs act as silent architects of our reality, building walls that confine our aspirations. These beliefs often manifest as self-doubt, fear of failure, or persistent feelings of inadequacy. Its impact is far-reaching, affecting various facets of our lives, from personal relationships to professional endeavors.

Self-sabotage and stagnation

One of the main consequences of limiting beliefs is self-sabotage. By internalizing notions of inadequacy or unworthiness, we inadvertently create a self-fulfilling prophecy, which hinders our progress and contributes to a cycle of stagnation.

Narrow perspectives

Limiting beliefs also narrow our perspectives, creating blind spots that prevent us from recognizing opportunities and possibilities. We become prisoners of our own mental constructs, unable to fully explore the vast landscape of potential around us.

Recognize limiting beliefs

The first step to freeing yourself from the chains of limiting beliefs is to recognize their presence. This process involves a conscious and courageous examination of our thoughts, feelings, and reactions to various situations.

Introspective research

Engaging in introspective research allows us to explore the beliefs that underpin our actions. Questions like "What do I believe about my abilities? or "What fears influence my decisions?" Open the door to self-discovery.

Pattern recognition

Limiting beliefs are often revealed through recurring patterns of thinking or behavior. Identifying these patterns provides valuable insight into deeply held beliefs that may be holding us back.

Unmask underlying beliefs

After recognizing the existence of limiting beliefs, the next phase is to unmask their underlying origins. These origins may be rooted in past experiences, social conditioning, or beliefs inherited from influential figures in our lives.

Return to the origin

Tracing the origins of limiting beliefs involves examining the formative experiences that may have contributed to their development. Whether they are rooted in childhood experiences, social expectations, or traumatic events, understanding the genesis of these beliefs is crucial to dismantling them.

Cultural and social influences

Beyond personal experiences, cultural and social influences play an important role in shaping our beliefs. Examining how social norms and expectations contribute to our belief system allows us to question and redefine those beliefs in alignment with our authentic self.

Tools to identify limiting beliefs

The journey toward identifying limiting beliefs is facilitated by a toolkit of practical strategies and exercises designed to raise awareness of these beliefs.

Login

Journaling provides a reflective space to document thoughts, emotions, and recurring patterns. Examining journal entries over time can reveal underlying limiting beliefs and patterns.

Mindfulness practices

Mindfulness practices, such as meditation and self-awareness exercises, cultivate present moment awareness. These practices allow people to observe their thoughts without judging them, revealing deeply held beliefs.

Professional orientation

Engaging with a mentor, coach, or therapist can provide valuable outside perspectives and guidance in identifying limiting beliefs. These people offer support in navigating the complex layers of one's belief system.

REWRITING THE NARRATIVE: TURNING LIMITS INTO OPPORTUNITIES

Identifying limiting beliefs is not a journey of self-flagellation but rather an empowerment process that paves the way for transformation. Once these beliefs have arisen into awareness, the next step is to rewrite the narrative, transforming perceived limitations into opportunities for growth.

Cropping techniques

Refaming techniques involve consciously questioning and reshaping limiting beliefs. By adopting a growth mindset and viewing challenges as opportunities for learning and development, people can reframe their perspective on limitations.

Visualization and affirmations

Visualization and positive affirmations are powerful tools for reprogramming the subconscious. By vividly imagining desired outcomes and affirming positive beliefs, people can overwrite limiting thought patterns.

Setting incremental goals

Setting and achieving incremental goals provides tangible proof of one's abilities, dismantling the illusion of limits. Small successes add up, gradually eroding the foundations of limiting beliefs.

The liberating power of self-discovery

In conclusion, the process of identifying limiting beliefs is a liberating journey of self-discovery. It is an expedition into the recesses of the mind, armed with the intention to reveal and dismantle the chains that hinder personal growth and success. This chapter serves as a guide and encourages readers to embark on this transformative odyssey, recognizing that the key to thriving lies in freeing ourselves from limiting beliefs that confine the limitless potential within us.

OVERCOME DOUBTS

At the crossroads of ambition and success is often the formidable obstacle of doubt. This insidious force, born from the shadows of our deepest insecurities, has the power to undermine our efforts, erode our confidence and cast a veil over our potential. Let us now embark on a journey to unmask the nature of doubt, exploring its origins and analyzing the mechanisms that make it a pervasive challenge on the path to prosperity.

The roots of doubt

Doubt, like a latent seed, often takes root in early experiences, social expectations, or critical moments of perceived failure. By digging deeper into the roots of self-doubt, readers gain insight into the specific triggers and narratives that contribute to this internal adversary.

Childhood influences

Childhood experiences, especially those that involve criticism or unmet expectations, can sow the seeds of insecurity. Understanding how early interactions shape self-perception is essential to overcoming deep-seated doubts.

Cultural and social pressures

Social norms and cultural expectations can create a breeding ground for doubt. Examining the impact of external pressures on individual beliefs allows for a nuanced understanding of the forces at play.

BUILDING THE ARMOR: STRATEGIES TO OVERCOME DOUBTS

Cultivate self-compassion

The basis for overcoming self-doubt is the practice of self-compassion. This means treating yourself with the same kindness and understanding that you would offer a friend facing similar challenges. Through exercises and reflections, readers learn to replace self-criticism with self-compassion.

Rewrite internal dialogue

The narrative we construct about ourselves often becomes a self-fulfilling prophecy. This section explores techniques for identifying and reshaping negative self-talk, allowing readers to transform their self-talk from critical to supportive ally.

Embracing imperfection: the path to authenticity

Perfectionism is a close companion to self-doubt, promoting an unattainable standard that fuels feelings of inadequacy. Accepting imperfection as a natural and beautiful aspect of the human experience becomes the cornerstone of the journey toward authenticity and self-acceptance.

Celebrate achievements big and small

In the quest to overcome self-doubt, recognizing and celebrating personal achievements, no matter how small, becomes a crucial practice. By acknowledging progress and successes, individuals build a reservoir of evidence that neutralizes the harmful effects of doubt.

THE ROLE OF MINDFULNESS: NAVIGATION IN THE PRESENT MOMENT

Mindfulness practices

Mindfulness, the practice of being fully present in the moment without judgment, appears to be a powerful tool for overcoming self-doubt. Techniques such as meditation, deep breathing, and mindfulness allow people to observe doubts without becoming entangled in their web.

Develop emotional resilience

Mindfulness not only improves present moment awareness, but also promotes emotional resilience. This resilience becomes a shield against the impact of self-doubt, allowing people to face challenges with a more stable and composed state of mind.

THE DOMINANT EFFECT: MAINTAIN A SUPPORTIVE ENVIRONMENT

In the complex dance of personal development and success, the importance of cultivating supportive relationships, fostering environments that foster growth, and distancing oneself from toxic influences cannot be overstated. This triad acts as the soil in which the seeds of our aspirations are planted, the climate that determines whether they thrive or wither. This article explores the deeper meaning of these interconnected elements, revealing the transformative power they have to shape our journey from difficulty to success.

CULTIVATE SUPPORTIVE RELATIONSHIPS: PILLARS OF ENCOURAGEMENT

Supportive relationships are pillars of encouragement in the tapestry of our lives. Whether they manifest as family ties, friendships, or professional relationships, these relationships form a network that supports and uplifts in times of challenge.

Emotional resilience

In times of adversity, having a support system provides a reservoir of emotional resilience. Supportive relationships provide a safe space for expression, validation, and reassurance that one is not alone in facing challenges.

Constructive feedback and growth

Constructive feedback from supportive relationships becomes a catalyst for growth. In a trusting environment, people are more likely to receive feedback openly, thus promoting continuous improvement and personal development.

PROMOTE ENVIRONMENTS THAT PROMOTE GROWTH

The power of the environment

Our immediate environments have a huge influence on our moods and behaviors. Fostering environments that encourage growth means creating spaces – both physical and mental – that nurture the seeds of ambition and potential.

An inspiring environment

Inspirational environments, whether through motivational quotes, art or a conducive workspace, stimulate creativity and ambition. Aesthetic and purpose-designed spaces contribute to a positive mood.

Learning opportunities

Environments that foster growth prioritize learning and development. Whether in the workplace, at home, or in social circles, an emphasis on continuous learning fuels a culture of improvement and innovation.

STAY AWAY FROM TOXIC INFLUENCES

Recognize toxicity

Toxic influences can seep into our lives in a variety of ways, from negative relationships to harmful habits. Recognizing toxicity is the first step to preserving well-being and creating space for positive growth.

Identify negative patterns

Negative behavior or communication patterns within relationships often indicate toxicity. Whether it's constant criticism, manipulation, or exhausting dynamics, recognizing these patterns is crucial for personal empowerment.

Set limits

Distancing yourself from toxic influences involves establishing firm, healthy boundaries. This may include limiting contact with people who constantly bring negativity or consciously choosing environments that align with our values.

THE SYMBIOSIS BETWEEN SUPPORT, GROWTH AND DISTANCE

Interconnected influence

All three elements (supportive relationships, growth-oriented environments, and distance from toxicity) work in symbiosis. Supportive relationships contribute to a positive environment, fostering personal growth, while distancing yourself from toxic influences is a form of self-preservation that nurtures both relationships and personal development.

The domino effect

The positive impact of nurturing supportive relationships and fostering growth-oriented environments extends outward. People who receive support and encouragement are more likely to return it, creating a cycle of positivity that extends beyond personal boundaries.

CHAPTER THREE

RESILIENCE IN ADVERSITY

Resilience in the face of adversity refers to the ability to recover, adapt and maintain well-being in the face of challenges, setbacks and difficult circumstances. It is a quality that allows people to face adversity, whether personal, professional or social, without succumbing to despair or feeling overwhelmed by current difficulties.

Key aspects of resilience in the face of adversity include:

1. **Adaptability:** Resilient people can adapt to changing situations and circumstances. They are flexible and willing to adjust their strategies, perspectives and behaviors to respond effectively to challenges.

2. **Emotional strength:** Resilience involves managing and regulating emotions effectively. It's not about repressing emotions, but about understanding them and managing them in a healthy way. This emotional strength helps people stay strong during difficult times.

3. **Optimism:** Resilient people tend to maintain a hopeful and optimistic attitude, even in the face of adversity. They

focus on possibilities and solutions rather than focusing only on problems.

4. **Problem-solving skills:** Resilience often involves a proactive approach to problem-solving. Resilient people are experts at analyzing situations, identifying possible solutions, and taking decisive action to address challenges.

5. **Social support:** Establishing and maintaining strong social connections is a crucial part of resilience. Having a support system provides emotional and practical help during difficult times, strengthening the individual's ability to cope.

6. **Self-reflection:** Resilient people engage in self-reflection, learn from their experiences, and use these lessons to grow and adapt. This reflection process helps them develop wisdom and strength over time.

7. **Sense of purpose:** Having a clear sense of purpose or meaning in life can contribute to resilience. People who understand their values and goals have a guiding force that helps them persevere in the face of adversity.

8. **Coping Strategies:** Resilient people generally have a repertoire of healthy coping strategies. These may include

mindfulness, exercise, seeking professional support, or participating in activities that bring joy and relaxation.

9. **Perseverance:** Resilience involves perseverance and the willingness to overcome challenges without giving up. It's about maintaining a long-term perspective and remaining committed to your goals, even in the midst of difficulties.

10. **Self-efficacy:** Resilient individuals have a sense of self-efficacy and believe in their ability to influence and overcome challenges. This confidence in their own abilities allows them to face adversity with determination.

Resilience is not a fixed characteristic but rather a dynamic quality that can be cultivated and strengthened over time. It is a valuable asset that contributes to personal growth, well-being and the ability to thrive in the face of life's inevitable difficulties.

NAVIGATING THE CHALLENGES

Challenges range from personal difficulties such as health problems or loss to professional obstacles such as career setbacks and financial difficulties. Recognizing the dynamic nature of challenges is essential, as this paves the way for developing coping strategies that meet the specific demands of each situation.

The inevitability of change

Challenges are often linked to changes, whether sudden or gradual. Meeting challenges requires recognizing the fluid nature of life and understanding that adaptability is a key asset in the face of changing circumstances.

THE ESSENCE OF RESILIENCE

Resilience is more than a buzzword; it is a deep psychological and emotional quality that allows individuals to recover from setbacks. Understanding the components of resilience – adaptability, emotional strength and perseverance – lays the foundation for effectively navigating through challenges.

BUILDING RESILIENCE: A LIFELONG PROCESS

Resilience is not a static trait but a dynamic skill that can be cultivated over time. This section explores strategies for building resilience, emphasizing the importance of self-awareness, positive coping mechanisms, and a growth mindset.

STRATEGIES TO ADDRESS CHALLENGES

Mindset and perception

The prism through which challenges are viewed greatly influences how they are approached. Adopting a growth mindset, viewing challenges as learning opportunities, and reframing adversity can have a profound impact on a person's ability to overcome obstacles.

Goal Setting and Planning

Strategic goal setting and planning provide a roadmap to address challenges. Breaking down larger challenges into smaller, manageable tasks and setting realistic, achievable goals promotes a sense of control and progress.

Emotional regulation

Addressing challenges effectively requires emotional regulation. This involves recognizing and understanding emotions, using coping mechanisms, and maintaining a balanced emotional state even in the face of adversity.

Welfare

Human connection is a powerful resource in times of challenge. Cultivating a support network, whether through friends, family or community, provides emotional support and practical assistance, thereby building resilience.

Learn from setbacks

Every challenge presents an opportunity for growth. Analyzing setbacks, identifying lessons learned, and incorporating that knowledge into one's approach fosters a continuous cycle of learning and adaptation.

CASE STUDIES AND REAL EXAMPLES

Inspiring Stories of Triumph

Examining real-life examples of individuals who overcome significant challenges and emerged triumphant provides tangible evidence of the transformative power of resilience. These case studies serve as beacons of inspiration, illustrating the various paths to overcoming adversity.

Commonalities of success stories

Identifying commonalities among success stories reveals recurring themes such as perseverance, adaptability and a positive mindset. These shared elements offer valuable information to individuals facing their own challenges.

CULTIVATE A RESILIENT CULTURE

Organizational and community resilience

Resilience principles extend beyond individual experiences to organizational and community levels. Fostering a resilient culture involves creating environments that support growth, collaboration and shared resilience.

Leadership and resilience

Leadership plays a vital role in overcoming challenges, whether in a professional or community setting. Effective leaders model resilience, inspire others, and create a supportive culture that enables collective triumph over adversity.

THE TRANSFORMATIVE POWER OF TRIUMPH

Personal growth and development

Meeting challenges is not simply about overcoming obstacles; It is a catalyst for growth and personal development. This section explores the transformative power of challenges, illustrating how resilience fosters strength, wisdom, and a deeper understanding of self.

Building the foundations for future success

Successfully overcoming challenges forms the basis for future success. The skills and knowledge acquired during the process become invaluable assets that enable individuals to face subsequent challenges with greater confidence and capability.

THE CURRENT JOURNEY: EMBRACE THE UNPREDICTABLE

Accept uncertainty

Life is inherently uncertain and challenges are intrinsic to the human experience. Accepting uncertainty becomes a mindset shift that allows people to approach challenges not as disruptions but as integral elements of a rich and dynamic existence.

The continuing evolution of resilience

Resilience is not a static achievement but a continuous evolution. As people face challenges, adapt and grow, their resilience goes through a process of transformation, becoming an steadfast companion in life's ongoing journey.

In short, overcoming challenges is a profound and transformative journey that encompasses the dynamic interplay of resilience, adaptability and triumph. By understanding the diverse nature of challenges, developing resilience as a lifelong skill, and employing strategic navigation strategies, individuals can transform adversity into an opportunity for growth. The triumph that comes from overcoming challenges goes beyond personal victories and contributes to the resilience of communities and organizations. By embracing the ongoing journey, people not only overcome challenges, but also emerge as architects of their own triumphs, exercising the transformative power of resilience within the complex canvas of life.

BUILDING INNER STRENGTH

Inner strength is not a rigid or singular quality; rather, it is a dynamic strength that encompasses mental, emotional, and spiritual resilience. It is the foundation to which people turn to face adversity, make decisions, and persevere in achieving their goals.

The interaction of mind, body and spirit

Developing inner strength involves recognizing the interconnectedness of mind, body, and spirit. A holistic approach considers the integration of mental well-being, emotional intelligence and a sense of purpose, fostering a strong foundation for personal empowerment.

THE PILLARS OF INTERNAL STRENGTH

Emotional resilience

Emotional resilience is a central pillar of inner strength. It involves the ability to adapt and recover from adversity, manage emotions effectively, and maintain a sense of balance even in difficult circumstances.

Strong minded

Mental toughness encompasses qualities such as focus, discipline and a positive mindset. Building mental toughness involves cultivating mental discipline, accepting challenges as opportunities for growth, and fostering a resilient thought process.

Compassion and self-love

Inner strength does not mean self-confidence at the expense of self-pity. Cultivating self-love and self-compassion forms the foundation of resilience, enabling people to meet challenges with gentleness and self-understanding.

Courage and confidence

Courage and confidence are the driving forces that push people to face their fears, take risks, and step out of their comfort zone. Developing inner strength involves fostering a sense of courage that allows people to face uncertainties with conviction.

Purpose and values

A clear sense of purpose and alignment with personal values contribute significantly to inner strength. Understanding one's purpose provides a guiding light, fostering a sense of purpose that builds resilience and determination.

STRATEGIES TO DEVELOP INNER STRENGTH

Mindfulness and self-awareness

Mindfulness practices and self-awareness play a key role in developing inner strength. Cultivating mindfulness allows people to be present in the moment, observe their thoughts without judgment, and develop a deeper understanding of themselves.

Positive affirmations and visualization

The power of positive affirmations and visualization cannot be underestimated. By consciously shaping positive beliefs about themselves and visualizing success, individuals develop inner strength and create a mental framework conducive to resilience.

Continuous learning and personal growth

Developing inner strength involves a commitment to continuous learning and personal growth. Accepting challenges as learning opportunities, seeking new experiences and expanding knowledge contribute to a resilient and adaptable mindset.

Gratitude Practices

Practicing gratitude is a transformative tool for developing inner strength. Focusing on the positive aspects of life and expressing gratitude for challenges and blessings fosters a resilient outlook capable of weathering the storms of adversity.

OVERCOME OBSTACLES TO INNER STRENGTH

Address self-doubt

Self-doubt can be a major barrier to developing inner strength. Recognizing and challenging self-doubt involves cultivating self-awareness, recognizing limiting beliefs, and reframing negative thoughts with positive affirmations.

Navigating fear and uncertainty

Fear and uncertainty are inherent to life, but they do not have to be obstacles to inner strength. Developing resilience in the face of fear involves recognizing emotions, reframing fear as a natural response to the unknown, and taking deliberate steps toward empowerment.

Manage stress and overwhelm

Effective stress management is crucial to maintaining inner strength. Strategies such as time management, prioritization, and incorporating relaxation techniques into daily routines contribute to a resilient approach to stress.

THE ROLE OF ADVERSITY IN THE DEVELOPMENT OF INNER STRENGTH

Accept adversity as a catalyst

Adversity is not an enemy but a catalyst for developing inner strength. Seeing challenges as opportunities for growth, reframing failures as learning experiences, and adapting to adversity all contribute to strengthening the inner core.

Resilience as a lifelong journey

Developing inner strength is not a destination but a lifelong journey. Accepting the ebb and flow of life, learning from experiences, and continually adapting to new challenges contribute to the continued development of inner resilience.

PERSONAL STORIES OF INNER STRENGTH

Inspiring stories

Exploring real-life stories of people who have demonstrated remarkable inner strength provides inspiration and tangible examples of resilience. These stories illustrate the various paths people take to develop inner strength in the face of adversity.

Common points of success stories

Identifying commonalities in success stories reveals recurring themes such as perseverance, self-confidence, and adaptability. These shared elements offer valuable information to people on their own journey towards building their inner strength.

PROMOTING A CULTURE OF INNER STRENGTH

Nurture the inner strength of others

Fostering inner strength goes beyond personal development to creating a culture that nurtures resilience in others. Whether in a family, community, or professional setting, cultivating environments that encourage self-discovery, support, and growth contributes to collective strength.

Educational and organizational practices

Educational institutions and organizations play a crucial role in developing inner strength. Implementing practices that promote emotional intelligence, mindfulness, and values-based leadership contributes to the development of resilient individuals and communities.

THE TRANSFORMATIVE POWER OF INNER FORCE

Personal empowerment and fulfillment

Developing inner strength is not just a way to cope with challenges; it is a path to personal empowerment and fulfillment. Individuals with inner strength are better equipped to face life's uncertainties with courage, resilience, and a sense of purpose.

Impact on well-being

The impact of inner strength on overall well-being is profound. Strong inner cores contribute to mental and emotional well-being, promoting a positive attitude and allowing individuals to navigate the complexities of life with a sense of balance.

CHAPTER FOUR

VISION AND CLARITY

Vision and clarity are interconnected concepts that play a crucial role in personal, professional and organizational success. They involve having a clear sense of direction, purpose and understanding that guides decision-making and actions.

VISION

1. **Definition:** Vision refers to a forward-looking, aspirational idea or concept that describes a desired future state. It is a mental image of what an individual, team or organization aims to achieve, often encompassing long-term goals and overarching aspirations.

2. **Features:**

• **Inspiration:** Vision inspires and motivates individuals by providing them with a compelling and positive picture of the future.

• **Alignment:** A well-defined vision aligns the efforts of individuals toward a common goal, fostering unity and collaboration.

• **Long-term goal:** The vision extends beyond short-term goals and summarizes the broader, enduring purpose of an entity.

3. **Significance:**

• **Guiding Principle:** Vision serves as a guiding principle, helping individuals make decisions and set priorities that align with long-term goals.

• **Motivation:** A clear and inspiring vision motivates individuals and teams, fostering a sense of purpose and engagement.

• **Strategic Direction:** The vision provides the strategic direction needed to address challenges and opportunities.

4. **Examples:**

• A company's vision statement describing its long-term goals and impact.

• An individual's personal vision for career growth and fulfillment.

CLARITY

1. **Definition:** Clarity involves the quality of being clear, consistent, and easy to understand. In the context of goals,

plans or communication, clarity ensures that there is no ambiguity, confusion or misunderstanding.

2. Features:

• **Precision:** Clarity involves precision in communication, making ideas and objectives easily understandable.

• **Simplicity:** Clear communication is often simple, avoiding unnecessary complexity that could lead to confusion.

• **Transparency:** Clarity promotes transparency, ensuring that information is accessible and easy to interpret.

3. Significance:

• **Effective communication:** Clarity of communication ensures that messages are conveyed accurately and that recipients understand the intended meaning.

• **Decision making:** Clear information is essential for informed decision making, reducing the risk of misunderstandings that can lead to errors.

• **Efficiency:** Clarity streamlines processes and actions, reducing the risk of errors or delays.

4. Examples:

• A well-structured project plan with clear objectives, timelines and responsibilities.

• A leader's clear and concise instructions to a team regarding a specific task.

VISION AND CLARITY TOGETHER

1. **Synergy:** Vision and clarity work in synergy. A clear vision needs clarity in communication to be effectively understood and adopted by individuals or teams.

2. **Implementation:** A visionary idea, when communicated clearly, facilitates successful implementation. Clear communication ensures that everyone understands their roles and responsibilities in achieving the vision.

3. **Alignment:** Clarity ensures that individuals and teams are aligned on the vision, understanding how their contributions fit into the larger picture.

In summary, vision provides the overall direction and purpose, while clarity ensures that the vision is effectively communicated, understood and implemented. Together, they create a powerful framework for achieving goals and fostering success in various aspects of life.

DEFINE YOUR GOAL

In the vast landscape of human existence, the quest for purpose is a lasting and profound effort. Defining your purpose is not just a journey; it is an odyssey of self-discovery, clarity and alignment with the deepest currents of your being.

THE ESSENCE OF PURPOSE

A guiding light

At its core, purpose serves as a guiding light, illuminating the path to a meaningful and fulfilling life. It encapsulates the deepest "why" of your actions, infusing every effort with a sense of meaning and resonance.

Intrinsic motivation

Purpose is a source of intrinsic motivation, providing the internal motivation necessary to overcome challenges and persevere in the pursuit of goals. It is the fuel that propels you in the face of obstacles and uncertainties.

THE JOURNEY OF SELF-DISCOVERY

Exploring values and beliefs

Defining your purpose involves an in-depth exploration of your values and beliefs. What matters most to you? What principles guide your decisions? Identifying these foundational elements is crucial to shaping a goal that authentically resonates with who you are.

Unearthing passions and talents

Passions and talents are an integral part of your purpose. Immersing yourself in activities that bring you joy and harnessing your unique talents unveils the natural inclinations that can be woven into the fabric of your purpose.

Align with core identity

Understanding your core identity is essential to defining your purpose. This involves recognizing your strengths, recognizing your vulnerabilities, and embracing your authentic self. Purpose aligns with your essence, fostering a feeling of congruence and authenticity.

THE TRANSFORMATIVE POWER OF PURPOSE

Improve well-being

Purpose has a profound impact on well-being. Studies show that individuals with a sense of purpose experience higher levels of life satisfaction, resilience, and overall psychological well-being.

Fueling Resilience

In the face of adversity, determination acts as a resilient force. It provides a framework for overcoming challenges, giving meaning to difficulties and allowing you to emerge stronger and more determined.

Inspiring action

The goal is not passive; it inspires intentional action. Whether it's personal relationships, career choices, or community involvement, a defined purpose becomes a catalyst for purposeful living and decision-making.

STRATEGIES FOR DEFINING YOUR GOAL

Reflection and introspection

Engaging in reflective practices and introspective inquiry opens the door to defining your purpose. Journaling, meditation, and introspection exercises create space for deeper self-awareness.

Looking for meaningful experiences

Actively seeking experiences that align with your values and passions makes it easier to discover purpose. Participate in various activities, explore new interests, and pay attention to what truly satisfies you.

Clarify goals and priorities

Aligning your goals and priorities with your values and vision helps define purpose. Clearly articulated goals become stepping stones on the path to a purpose-driven life.

Learn from the challenges

Challenges are not obstacles but opportunities for growth and development. Facing challenges with a growth mindset allows you to draw valuable lessons that contribute to the evolution of your goal.

ADAPTING A GOAL IN DIFFERENT AREAS OF LIFE

Race goal

In the professional sphere, defining your purpose involves aligning your career with your values, thus contributing to a feeling of fulfillment and meaning in your work. This involves understanding the impact you want to have on your profession and the world at large.

Personal relationships

Purpose extends to personal relationships, influencing how you interact with others. Cultivating purpose in relationships involves fostering meaningful connections, contributing to the well-being of loved ones, and creating a support network.

Community and social objective

Contributing to the community and society as a whole adds a community dimension to the goal. Engaging in social causes, volunteering, or advocating for meaningful change reflects a motivated commitment to making a positive impact beyond the individual sphere.

OVERCOME OBSTACLES TOWARDS THE GOAL

Facing fear and uncertainty

Fear and uncertainty can be obstacles on the path to goal setting. Recognizing these emotions, reframing them as natural responses to the unknown, and taking gradual steps can help overcome these obstacles.

Manage external expectations

External expectations, whether from society, family, or cultural norms, can obscure clarity of purpose. Setting boundaries and aligning decisions with personal values helps you cope with external pressures and stay true to your goal.

Embrace evolution

The goal is not static; evolves over time. Accepting the fluid nature of purpose allows for growth, adaptation, and integration of new knowledge and experiences into the evolving narrative of your life's purpose.

THE ROLE OF MENTORING AND GUIDANCE

Seeking mentorship

Connecting with mentors or seeking advice from those who have been through a similar journey can offer valuable insights and perspectives. Mentors provide support, share wisdom, and facilitate the discovery of purpose.

Professional orientation

Career guidance, whether from career counselors or life coaches, can provide structured frameworks and tools to define your purpose. Working with expert professionals to guide people in exploring goals can provide valuable support.

SUPPORT A GOAL THROUGH DAILY PRACTICES

Daily rituals and habits

Incorporating purpose-aligned rituals and habits into daily life strengthens your connection to your purpose. Whether through morning routines, mindfulness practices, or intentional acts of kindness, these habits contribute to a purposeful existence.

Periodic reflection

Reflecting on your purpose regularly ensures that it remains a dynamic and evolving force in your life. Setting aside time for introspection allows you to recalibrate your goals, align your actions with your purpose, and stay in tune with your deepest motivations.

In short, defining your goal is not a destination but an ongoing search for meaning and fulfillment. It involves a lifelong journey of self-discovery, aligning with values and translating aspirations into intentional actions. Purpose serves as a guiding force, lighting the way even in the face of uncertainty and challenges.

SET CLEAR GOALS: A STRATEGIC PLAN FOR SUCCESS AND FULFILLMENT

In the search for personal and professional excellence, the art of setting clear objectives is a fundamental pillar. The process of defining, articulating and pursuing well-defined goals is more than a routine task; It is a strategic plan that leads people toward success and fulfillment.

THE ESSENCE OF CLEAR OBJECTIVES

Setting clear goals involves the deliberate process of articulating goals that are specific, measurable, achievable, relevant and time-bound. These goals serve as guideposts that provide direction and purpose while creating a roadmap for progress.

Clarity as a catalyst

The clarity inherent in well-defined goals acts as a catalyst for motivation and focused action. It provides a tangible goal, makes aspirations more achievable, and fosters a sense of purpose that guides decision-making and priority setting.

THE PSYCHOLOGY OF GOAL SETTING

Motivation and direction

Clear goals are powerful motivators, generating a sense of purpose that moves people forward. They provide direction, align efforts toward a defined end goal, and inspire commitment to action.

Goal Setting Theory

Psychological theories, such as Edwin Locke's goal-setting theory, emphasize the profound impact of clear goals on performance and satisfaction. The theory posits that specific, challenging goals lead to higher levels of performance when combined with engagement, feedback, and task complexity.

STRATEGIES FOR SETTING CLEAR OBJECTIVES

SMART criteria

Meeting SMART criteria (specific, measurable, achievable, relevant, time-bound) is a fundamental strategy in goal setting. This framework ensures that goals are well-defined, realistic and aligned with broader aspirations.

Distribution and prioritization

Breaking down larger goals into smaller, more achievable tasks improves clarity and facilitates a step-by-step approach. Prioritization ensures that efforts are directed toward high-impact goals, avoiding overload and promoting efficiency.

Alignment with values

Setting goals that align with personal values improves intrinsic motivation. When goals align with core beliefs and aspirations, people are more likely to stay engaged and find deeper meaning in their goals.

Periodic review and adjustment

Periodic review of objectives allows for reflection and adjustment. As circumstances change or new knowledge emerges, the ability to adapt goals ensures continued relevance and alignment with evolving aspirations.

THE TRANSFORMATIVE POWER OF ACHIEVING GOALS

Feeling of triumph

Achieving goals brings a deep sense of accomplishment. Whether big or small, each step taken contributes to a positive feedback loop, building confidence in one's abilities.

Motivational dynamism

Success breeds success: Achieving goals creates a motivation boost that pushes people to tackle subsequent challenges with more confidence and determination.

Continued growth

Goal setting is intrinsically linked to personal growth. Achieving goals requires learning, adapting and developing new skills, contributing to a continuous evolution of capabilities.

OVERCOMING OBSTACLES IN GOAL SETTING

Address the fear of failure

Fear of failure can make it difficult to set goals. Adopting a growth mindset, viewing failures as learning opportunities, and understanding that setbacks are inherent in pursuing ambitious goals helps overcome this obstacle.

Navigating Procrastination

Procrastination is a common challenge in achieving goals. Breaking tasks into smaller, more manageable steps, setting realistic deadlines, and leveraging accountability mechanisms are effective strategies for overcoming procrastination.

Managing unrealistic expectations

Setting goals that are too ambitious can lead to burnout and disappointment. Setting realistic goals involves taking into account current capabilities, resources and time constraints, to ensure that goals are ambitious but achievable.

SETTING GOALS IN VARIOUS AREAS OF LIFE

Career and professional goals

In the professional field, establishing clear objectives is essential to advance in your career. Articulating short- and long-term goals, skill development and milestones contributes to a strategic and focused career path.

Personal development and well-being

Wellbeing and personal development goals cover areas such as physical health, mental wellbeing and personal development. These goals improve overall life satisfaction and contribute to a balanced and satisfying lifestyle.

Relationships and communication

Clear relationship goals involve effective communication, mutual growth, and shared aspirations. Setting goals for communication, quality time, and collaborative efforts strengthens the foundation for meaningful relationships.

THE ROLE OF VISUALIZATION AND AFFIRMATION

Visualization techniques

Visualization involves mentally imagining the success of goals. This technique improves motivation, promotes a positive mindset, and mentally prepares people for the challenges and triumphs along the way.

Affirmations for positive reinforcement

Positive affirmations are statements that build confidence in one's own abilities and in achieving one's goals. Regularly incorporating affirmations into daily routines improves self-confidence, resilience and a constructive attitude.

CULTIVATE RESILIENCE IN THE PURSUIT OF GOALS

Accept setbacks

Resilience is vital in the face of setbacks. Viewing challenges as temporary obstacles, learning from failures, and adapting strategies contribute to a resilient mindset that maintains motivation in the face of adversity.

Learning orientation

A learning orientation involves viewing goals as opportunities for growth rather than fixed reference points. Showing curiosity to learn, adapt and iterate improves resilience and promotes a positive approach to challenges.

SETTING OBJECTIVES IN A COLLABORATIVE CONTEXT

Organizational and team goals

In organizational and team contexts, clear goals align efforts, promote collaboration, and provide a sense of common purpose. Articulating collective objectives improves cohesion and promotes collective success.

Leadership and goal alignment

Effective leadership involves aligning organizational goals with individual and collective aspirations. Clear communication, regular feedback and creating a culture that values goal setting contributes to a motivated and engaged workforce.

THE HOLISTIC IMPACT OF GOAL SETTING

Balancing Multiple Goals

People often juggle multiple goals in various areas of life. Achieving balance involves effective time management, prioritization and periodic reassessment of goals to ensure alignment with overall aspirations.

Preventing burnout

Burnout can occur when people relentlessly pursue their goals without taking care of themselves. Taking advantage of breaks, celebrating small victories and maintaining a realistic pace contribute to sustained motivation and well-being.

LIFE'S JOURNEY TO SET GOALS

Evolving aspirations

Goal setting is a dynamic process that evolves with changing circumstances and aspirations. Embracing goal fluidity allows people to adapt to new opportunities and ideas that arise over time.

Reflection and celebration

Reflecting on goal achievement is an integral part of the goal setting process. Celebrating successes, expressing gratitude for progress, and recognizing personal growth all contribute to a positive and rewarding experience.

In short, setting clear goals is not a simple task, but a transformative journey that shapes the narrative of a fulfilling and purposeful life. The process involves self-discovery, resilience, and a commitment to continued growth. Well-defined goals act as compass points, guiding people through the complexities of personal and professional landscapes.

CHAPTER FIVE

MENTALITY CHANGE

A mindset shift, also known as mindset shift or mindset shift, refers to a fundamental change in the way an individual perceives, thinks and approaches various aspects of life, challenges, opportunities and beliefs. It involves a transformation of the underlying set of attitudes, beliefs and assumptions that shape a person's understanding and reactions to the world.

Key aspects of a mindset shift include:

1. **Change in perspective:** A change in mindset often involves seeing situations, challenges or opportunities from a different perspective. This may require challenging existing beliefs and adopting new ways of thinking.

2. **Adopt a growth mindset:** A common type of mindset change is transitioning from a fixed mindset to a growth mindset. In a growth mindset, people believe that their abilities and intelligence can develop through dedication, effort, and learning, rather than becoming fixed traits.

3. **Accept change and uncertainty:** Changing your way of thinking means becoming more comfortable with change

and uncertainty. Instead of fearing the unknown, people with an altered mindset can see it as an opportunity for growth and learning.

4. **Overcome limiting beliefs:** Mindset changes often involve identifying and challenging limiting beliefs that may be holding people back. This may include self-doubt, fear of failure, or other negative thought patterns.

5. **Cultivate positive thinking:** A change in mindset can involve consciously cultivating positive thinking and focusing on solutions instead of dwelling on problems. This can contribute to a more optimistic and resilient outlook.

6. **Develop a solution-focused approach:** Changing your mindset often means moving from a problem-focused approach to a solution-focused mindset. Instead of dwelling on obstacles, people with an altered mindset actively look for ways to overcome challenges.

7. **Improve emotional intelligence:** A change in mindset can involve improving emotional intelligence, which includes self-awareness, self-regulation, empathy, and effective interpersonal relationships.

8. **Seeing failure as feedback:** Instead of seeing failure as an end result, a change in mindset involves seeing it as a

valuable source of feedback and an opportunity to learn and grow.

9. **Openness to continuous learning:** People with a changed mindset adopt a continuous learning mindset. They understand that knowledge evolves and that remaining open to new information and ideas is essential for their personal and professional development.

10. **Take responsibility and take responsibility:** A change in mindset often involves taking responsibility for your actions, choices, and results. Instead of playing the role of victim, people with an altered mindset recognize their agency and responsibility.

Mindset changes are powerful because they can lead to positive changes in behavior, decision making, and overall well-being. Although cultivating it requires time and effort, the impact of a change in mindset can be profound, influencing various aspects of an individual's life and contributing to their personal and professional success.

CULTIVATE A PROSPEROUS MINDSET: FOSTER ABUNDANCE AND SUCCESS FROM WITHIN

In the complex landscape of personal development, the concept of a thriving mindset is emerging as a transformative force that shapes the way people perceive, approach and navigate life's journey. Cultivating a prosperous mindset involves fostering a mindset that aligns with abundance, success, and a sense of fulfillment.

DEFINING A PROSPEROUS MINDSET

Embrace Abundance

At its core, a thriving mindset is based on the belief in abundance. It is a mindset that views opportunities, resources, and possibilities as abundant, not scarce. This change in perception lays the foundation for a positive and proactive approach to life.

Align yourself with success

A fulfilled mindset aligns with success and prosperity on various levels, whether it be personal achievements, professional endeavors, or overall life satisfaction. This involves fostering belief in one's own ability to create and attract success in different facets of life.

Holistic wellness

Cultivating a prosperous mindset goes beyond material success. It encompasses holistic wellness, emphasizing mental, emotional and spiritual abundance as integral components of a prosperous life.

BASIC PRINCIPLES OF A PROSPEROUS MINDSET

Positive affirmation

Positive affirmations play a crucial role in developing a thriving mindset. These are intentional, positive statements that individuals repeat to themselves, reinforcing their beliefs in abundance, success, and self-worth.

Gratitude practices

Gratitude is the cornerstone of a thriving mindset. Regularly recognizing and appreciating the abundance of life, whether big or small, promotes a positive attitude and attracts more positive experiences.

Growth mindset

A growth mindset is essential to cultivating prosperity. This mindset views challenges as opportunities for growth, welcomes learning, and believes in the ability to develop skills and overcome obstacles.

Visualization techniques

Visualization involves mentally imagining yourself achieving your desired goals and experiencing success. This technique enhances belief systems, focuses the mind on positive outcomes, and attracts opportunities aligned with expected success.

STRATEGIES TO CULTIVATE A THRIVING MINDSET

Personal reflection and awareness

Self-reflection encourages awareness of existing thought patterns and beliefs. Cultivating a thriving mindset starts with understanding and challenging any limiting beliefs that may get in the way of a positive outlook.

Surround yourself with positivity

The environment plays an important role in the development of the state of mind. Actively choosing to surround yourself with positive influences, whether through relationships, media consumption, or your daily environment, contributes to a fulfilled state of mind.

Set and pursue inspiring goals

Goals that align with individual passions and values contribute to a fulfilled state of mind. Setting inspiring goals and actively pursuing them gives life purpose, direction and a sense of accomplishment.

Act inspired

A thriving mindset is not passive; It involves taking inspired and intentional action to achieve goals. Proactivity and the willingness to step out of comfort zones contribute to the manifestation of abundance.

OVERCOME LIMITING BELIEFS

Identify and challenge limiting beliefs

Limiting beliefs, such as thoughts of scarcity or doubt, can prevent the development of a thriving mindset. Identifying and challenging these beliefs involves reframing negative thoughts and replacing them with empowering thoughts.

Adopt a positive self-image

Self-perception plays a crucial role in the development of mindset. Cultivating a fulfilled state of mind involves adopting a positive self-image, recognizing your strengths and promoting self-compassion.

Learn from failures

Setbacks are part of the journey, but a thriving mindset views them as opportunities to learn and grow. Instead of viewing failure as an end result, people with a thriving mindset learn from it and adjust their approach.

APPLY THE PRINCIPLES OF PROSPERITY TO DIFFERENT AREAS OF LIFE

Financial prosperity

In finance, a thriving mindset involves adopting healthy financial habits, believing in financial abundance, and making decisions aligned with long-term prosperity rather than short-term gains.

Career and professional success

Cultivating a thriving mindset in a professional context involves setting career goals, believing in your abilities, and approaching challenges with a solutions-focused mindset. Networking and finding growth opportunities contribute to professional prosperity.

Relationships and connection

Prosperity extends to relationships by fostering positive connections. A thriving relationship mindset involves empathy, effective communication, and a belief in abundant love, support, and meaningful relationships.

MAINTAINING RESILIENCE WITH A THRIVING MINDSET

Resilience in adversity

A prosperous mindset is resilient in the face of adversity. Instead of succumbing to challenges, people with a prosperity mindset view setbacks as temporary and use them as stepping stones to future success.

Positive response to change

Change is inevitable and a thriving mindset responds positively to it. Accepting change as an opportunity for growth, adaptation and new possibilities contributes to a perspective of resilience and prosperity.

THE ROLE OF THE COMMUNITY AND SUPPORT

Building a thriving community

Cultivating a thriving mindset is enhanced by being part of a community that shares similar values and aspirations. Joining groups, participating in support networks, and seeking mentorship all contribute to a shared journey toward prosperity.

Mutual support and encouragement

Mutual support within a community or between friends and family is essential. Mutual encouragement fosters a sense of shared prosperity, in which individuals encourage each other in the pursuit of common and individual goals.

THE LIFE JOURNEY OF A PROSPEROUS MINDSET

Continuous growth and evolution

Cultivating a thriving mindset is a lifelong journey of continuous growth and evolution. Embracing change, staying open to new possibilities, and adapting your mindset to changing circumstances all contribute to a prosperous and fulfilling life.

Reflection on achievements

Regularly reflecting on achievements and expressing gratitude for progress strengthens the thriving mindset. Celebrating successes, no matter how small, contributes to having a positive and motivated attitude.

In short, cultivating a thriving mindset is a profound journey that takes place in the areas of belief, action, and energy that individuals bring to their lives. It's about embracing abundance, fostering positive thought patterns, and taking intentional steps toward success and fulfillment.

POSITIVE AFFIRMATIONS: HARNESSING THE POWER OF POSITIVE SELF-TALK FOR TRANSFORMATION

Within the complex framework of personal development and mental well-being, positive affirmations emerge as powerful tools, capable of shaping thoughts, beliefs and actions. These intentional statements, when repeated constantly, have the potential to rewire the subconscious, promoting a positive mindset and influencing the trajectory of life.

UNDERSTANDING POSITIVE AFFIRMATIONS

Positive affirmations are concise, positive statements that people repeat to themselves with the goal of instilling positive beliefs, fostering empowerment, and cultivating a constructive mindset. These affirmations serve as statements of self-esteem, abilities, and achievement of desired results.

The power of language

Language is a powerful force that shapes thoughts and beliefs. Positive affirmations harness the power of words to redirect internal narratives, replacing self-limiting or negative thoughts with empowering and optimistic perspectives.

FUNDAMENTAL PRINCIPLES OF POSITIVE AFFIRMATIONS

Statement structure

Creating effective positive affirmations involves structuring the statements in the present tense, using positive language, and phrasing them as if the desired outcome is already happening. This approach reinforces the sense of immediacy and inevitability.

Personalization

Effective positive affirmations are personal and resonant. Tailoring statements to reflect individual goals, values, and aspirations strengthens their impact, creating a deep connection between the statement and the individual's authentic self.

Repetition and consistency

Repetition is a key part of positive affirmations. Constant repetition reinforces desired beliefs, gradually replacing ingrained negative thought patterns with affirmative, constructive thought patterns.

Emotional resonance

For positive affirmations to have impact, they must evoke positive emotions. Connecting emotionally to statements improves their effectiveness, because emotions play an important role in forming belief systems.

THE TRANSFORMATIVE IMPACT OF POSITIVE AFFIRMATIONS

Mentality change

Positive affirmations serve as catalysts for mindset changes. They inspire people to challenge their limiting beliefs and cultivate a more optimistic, growth-oriented perspective.

Strengthen confidence and self-esteem.

Constantly using positive affirmations helps build confidence and self-esteem. Affirming one's abilities and worth promotes a positive self-image, allowing people to face challenges with confidence.

Stress reduction

Positive affirmations can relieve stress by redirecting attention from negative thoughts to the affirmations. This shift in mental focus promotes a sense of calm and resilience in the face of challenges.

STRATEGIES TO EFFECTIVELY USE POSITIVE AFFIRMATIONS

Goal Alignment

Aligning affirmations with specific goals improves their effectiveness. Crafting statements that align with desired outcomes strengthens the link between belief and success.

Visualization techniques

Combining positive affirmations with visualization techniques amplifies their impact. Imagining the desired results while affirming their achievement creates a powerful synergy between thought and mental images.

Affirmation rituals

Incorporating affirmations into daily rituals, such as morning routines or bedtime rituals, establishes consistency. Constant practice reinforces positive messages and gradually ingrains them in the subconscious.

Affirmation Journal

Keeping an affirmation journal provides a tangible record of positive thoughts and progress. Journaling allows people to reflect on their journey, track mindset changes, and celebrate successes.

OVERCOMING THE CHALLENGES OF PRACTICING POSITIVE AFFIRMATION

Dealing with resistance

Resistance to positive affirmations can arise due to deeply held negative beliefs. Recognizing resistance and persistently engaging in affirmations can gradually break down barriers and foster acceptance.

Adjust assertions

Adapting statements according to changing objectives or circumstances ensures their relevance. Periodic reassessment and adjustment contribute to long-lasting effectiveness.

Balancing realism and positivity

Positive affirmations should strike a balance between positivity and realism. While they encourage optimism, they must also align with achievable goals and be anchored in a belief system that feels authentic.

APPLY POSITIVE AFFIRMATIONS IN ALL AREAS OF LIFE

Personal growth and development

In the area of personal growth, positive affirmations support the journey of self-discovery, lifelong learning, and developing new skills. Affirming your ability to grow fosters a growth mindset.

Relationships and communication

Positive affirmations play a role in promoting positive relationships. Affirming one's own qualities and expressing gratitude for the positive aspects of others contributes to a healthy and supportive social environment.

Career and professional success

Professionally, positive affirmations can build confidence, build resilience in the face of challenges, and cultivate a success-oriented mindset. The affirmation of professional capabilities contributes to professional development.

THE ROLE OF AFFIRMATIONS IN MENTAL HEALTH

Manage negative thought patterns

Positive affirmations are a valuable tool for managing negative thought patterns associated with anxiety, depression, or low self-esteem. Affirmations redirect focus and promote more constructive thinking.

Improve resilience

Affirmations contribute to resilience by fostering a mindset that can withstand adversity. Regular practice builds mental strength and helps people bounce back stronger after setbacks.

Promote self-compassion

Affirmations that emphasize self-compassion and self-love contribute to mental well-being. Recognizing and affirming your own value promotes a positive relationship with yourself.

THE SCIENCE BEHIND POSITIVE STATEMENTS

Neuroplasticity

The concept of neuroplasticity supports the effectiveness of positive affirmations. Neuroplasticity refers to the brain's ability to reorganize itself, and affirmations help reconfigure the neural pathways associated with beliefs and behaviors.

Impact on stress hormones

Research suggests that positive affirmations can affect stress hormones such as cortisol. Engaging in positive self-talk has been linked to lower stress levels and greater resilience.

Link to cognitive behavioral therapy (CBT)

Positive affirmations share similarities with cognitive behavioral therapy (CBT) techniques. Both focus on challenging and changing negative thought patterns to promote emotional well-being and positive behavior.

THE ROLE OF THE COMMUNITY AND SUPPORT

Shared Affirmation Practices

Engaging in affirming practices within a community or with a support network improves their impact. Shared affirmations create collective energy that reinforces positive beliefs and encourages mutual growth.

Peer Accountability

Partners or accountability groups can provide motivation and encouragement for consistent affirmation practice. Shared experiences and progress contribute to a sense of community and shared success.

A LIFETIME JOURNEY OF POSITIVE AFFIRMATIONS

Continued growth and adaptation

Positive affirmations are not static; They evolve with individuals as they grow and change. Embracing the fluidity of affirmation practice allows for continued adaptation to new goals and aspirations.

Reflection and celebration

Reflecting on the impact of positive affirmations and celebrating personal growth strengthens their effectiveness. Recognizing progress contributes to a positive feedback loop, which encourages continued practice.

In short, positive affirmations are powerful instruments of personal transformation, offering people a path to reshape their thoughts, their beliefs, and ultimately their lives. As people move toward integrating positive affirmations into their daily practices, they unlock the transformative potential of positive, intentional self-talk.

CHAPTER SIX

FINANCIAL EMPOWERMENT

Financial empowerment refers to the process and state of taking control of one's financial situation, making informed financial decisions, and developing the knowledge, skills, and confidence needed to effectively manage and improve one's well-being financial. This is a multi-faceted concept that goes beyond a certain amount of money; This encompasses financial education, self-sufficiency and the ability to take actions that lead to financial security and independence.

Key elements of financial empowerment include:

1. **Financial Literacy:** Understanding basic financial concepts such as budgeting, saving, investing, debt management and financial planning is essential to financial empowerment. Financial education provides the foundation for making informed money decisions.

2. **Budgeting and money management:** Financial empowerment involves creating and sticking to a budget. This includes tracking income and expenses, setting

financial goals, and allocating resources in a way that aligns with one's priorities.

3. **Debt Management:** Effectively managing and reducing debt is an essential aspect of financial empowerment. This may involve strategies such as debt consolidation, negotiating interest rates, and creating a plan to pay off outstanding balances.

4. **Savings and investments:** Generating savings and making informed investment decisions contribute to financial empowerment. Having an emergency fund for unexpected expenses and understanding how to grow your wealth through investments is key.

5. **Income Generation:** Seeking opportunities to increase income, whether through career advancement, side hustles, or entrepreneurship, is part of financial empowerment. This means actively seeking paths to financial growth and stability.

6. **Financial Planning:** Developing a comprehensive financial plan involves setting short- and long-term goals, identifying strategies to achieve them, and adapting the plan as circumstances change. Financial empowerment means having a roadmap for the future.

7. **Risk management and insurance:** Understanding and managing financial risks, such as health problems or unexpected events, is essential. This may involve having adequate insurance coverage to protect you against unforeseen circumstances.

8. **Negotiation skills:** Negotiating financial matters, such as salaries, commissions or interest rates, is a skill that contributes to financial empowerment. Being able to stand up for yourself in financial transactions is empowering.

9. **Financial Confidence:** Financial empowerment is also about building confidence in one's ability to navigate the financial landscape. It involves overcoming financial fears, taking calculated risks, and learning from successes and failures.

10. **Creating Generational Wealth:** Financial empowerment often extends to the goal of creating and passing on wealth to future generations. This may involve estate planning, investing, and financial responsibility education.

11. **Access to resources:** Having access to financial resources, whether in the form of educational materials, tools or support networks, is crucial for financial

empowerment. This includes staying informed about financial trends and opportunities.

Financial empowerment is a dynamic and continuous process. It is not just about accumulating wealth, but also about developing a mindset and skills that enable people to make sound financial decisions, adapt to changing circumstances and achieve their financial goals. Ultimately, financial empowerment provides people with the tools and autonomy to shape their financial destiny and work toward a more secure and fulfilling future.

SMART MONEY HABITS: A COMPLETE GUIDE TO FINANCIAL WELL-BEING

In the complex environment of personal finance, developing smart financial habits is the cornerstone of financial well-being and security. These habits encompass a variety of behaviors, attitudes, and strategies that enable people to make informed financial decisions, manage their resources effectively, and achieve their short- and long-term financial goals.

UNDERSTANDING SMART MONEY HABITS

Smart financial habits are intentional strategic actions that people consistently practice to optimize their financial health. These habits cover a wide range of financial behaviors, from budgeting and saving to investing and planning for the future. At its core, smart financial habits are about making thoughtful decisions that align with our financial goals and values.

Holistic financial management

Smart financial habits go beyond isolated financial transactions; They involve a holistic approach to financial management. This involves mastering budgeting skills, developing a savings mindset, investing wisely, managing debt effectively, and planning for long-term financial success.

BASICS OF SMART MONEY HABITS

Financial education

Financial education is one of the foundations of intelligent financial habits. This involves understanding key financial concepts, terms and strategies. An educated person is better equipped to make informed decisions about their money and investments.

Proactive planning

Smart financial habits incorporate proactive planning. This involves setting financial goals, creating budgets, and developing comprehensive financial plans that guide decision-making and resource allocation.

Conscious spending

Spending mindfully is a crucial part of smart financial habits. This involves being conscious of how money is spent, prioritizing needs over wants, and making intentional decisions to avoid unnecessary spending.

Creating emergency funds

Creating and maintaining an emergency fund is a key smart money habit. This financial cushion provides a safety net for unexpected expenses, providing peace of mind and avoiding the need to resort to high-interest debt in an emergency.

IMPLEMENT SMART MONEY HABITS INTO DAILY LIFE ESTIMATE

Creating and sticking to a budget is the cornerstone of good financial habits. Budgets provide a road map for managing income and expenses, allowing people to allocate resources effectively and avoid overspending.

Save strategically

Smart financial habits include strategic saving. This involves saving consistently, automating savings contributions, and taking advantage of tools like employer-sponsored retirement accounts, individual retirement accounts (IRAs), and other savings vehicles.

Debt management

Effectively managing and minimizing debt is a key smart money habit. This may involve paying off high-interest debt, consolidating loans, and avoiding accumulating unnecessary debt through prudent financial decision-making.

Investment strategies

Making strategic investments is the hallmark of smart financial habits. This may include diversifying investment portfolios, staying informed of market trends, and aligning investments with long-term financial goals and risk tolerance.

Continuous learning

Smart financial habits are dynamic and respond to changing financial landscapes. Continuous learning about personal finance, investment strategies and economic trends is a habit that allows people to adapt and make informed decisions.

THE TRANSFORMATIVE IMPACT OF SMART MONEY HABITS

Financial stability

Consistently following smart financial habits contributes to financial stability. By building a solid foundation of financial education, planning and responsible decision-making, people improve their overall financial well-being.

Living without debt

Effective debt management is a key outcome of smart financial habits. People who prioritize debt reduction and avoid unnecessary borrowing enjoy greater financial freedom and reduce the financial stress associated with debt.

Accumulation of wealth

Smart financial habits play a crucial role in wealth accumulation. Through strategic saving, investing and long-term financial planning, people can build wealth and achieve financial goals.

STRATEGIES FOR CULTIVATING AND MAINTAINING SMART MONEY HABITS

Define aims

Setting clear, achievable financial goals is a strategy for cultivating smart financial habits. These goals provide direction, motivation and a framework for decision making.

Financial Automation

Automating financial processes, such as savings contributions and bill payments, streamlines money management. Automation reduces the likelihood of payment defaults and encourages consistent savings.

Periodic financial controls

Performing regular financial check-ins is one strategy for maintaining smart financial habits. Regular reviews of budgets, objectives and investment portfolios allow for adjustments and ensure alignment with changing circumstances.

Seek professional advice

Engaging with financial advisors or seeking professional advice is a prudent strategy. Financial experts can provide personalized advice, address specific concerns and help people make informed decisions based on their particular financial situation.

OVERCOME THE CHALLENGES OF DEVELOPING SMART HOME HABITS

Fight against impulsive spending

Impulsive spending challenges smart financial habits. To address this challenge, it is necessary to practice mindfulness, create spending plans, and establish mechanisms to pause and reconsider unplanned purchases.

Manage lifestyle inflation

As income increases, there may be a tendency for spending to increase, known as lifestyle inflation. Smart financial habits involve resisting unnecessary lifestyle inflation and prioritizing long-term financial goals over immediate gratification.

Navigating economic uncertainty

Economic uncertainties, such as market fluctuations or job insecurity, can be difficult. Smart financial habits include having contingency plans, maintaining emergency funds, and staying focused on long-term financial goals despite short-term fluctuations.

APPLY SMART MONEY HABITS IN ALL AREAS OF LIFE

Family finances

Smart financial habits extend to family finances, involving open communication about financial goals, joint decision-making, and collaborative efforts to build a secure financial future.

Education and lifelong learning

Instilling smart financial habits in education involves teaching financial knowledge from a young age. Lifelong learning about personal finance ensures that people remain informed and adaptable throughout their lives.

Retirement planning

Retirement planning is an important aspect of smart financial habits. This includes contributing to retirement accounts, exploring investment opportunities, and adjusting retirement plans as circumstances change.

THE ROLE OF SMART FINANCIAL HABITS IN ECONOMIC EMPOWERMENT

Breaking financial cycles

Smart financial habits break negative financial cycles. People who cultivate these habits can free themselves from cycles of debt, overspending, and financial instability, paving the way to economic empowerment.

Create generational wealth

Smart financial habits help build generational wealth. By instilling financial literacy and responsible financial management in younger generations, families can create a legacy of financial empowerment.

Economic mobility

Adopting smart financial habits influences economic mobility. People who prioritize financial education, savings, and strategic decision making improve their ability to move up the economic ladder.

A LIFETIME JOURNEY OF SMART MONEY HABITS

Scalable financial goals

Smart financial habits adapt to changes in financial goals. As people go through different stages of life, the nature of their financial goals may change, requiring adjustments to their financial management strategies.

Generational impact

The impact of smart financial habits spans generations. Families that prioritize financial education and responsible financial behaviors influence the financial well-being of future generations.

Continuous refinement

Smart financial habits involve continuous refinement. Regular assessments, learning from experience, and adapting strategies contribute to continued financial growth and well-being.

In short, developing smart financial habits is not just a set of behaviors; It is a transformative journey towards financial fulfillment. By integrating the principles of financial literacy, proactive planning, and strategic decision-making into daily life, people are empowered to confidently navigate the complexities of personal finances.

CREATING MULTIPLE INCOME STREAMS: A STRATEGIC APPROACH TO FINANCIAL ABUNDANCE

In the dynamic personal finance landscape, the concept of creating multiple income streams presents itself as a powerful strategy for achieving financial abundance and resilience.

UNDERSTANDING MULTIPLE SOURCES OF INCOME

Definition and essence

Creating multiple income streams means generating income from multiple sources, beyond a traditional salary or primary activity. These streams can include secondary activities, investments, royalties, passive income and other means that contribute to a diversified and resilient financial portfolio.

Diversification as a financial strategy

The essence of creating multiple income streams lies in the principle of diversification. Similar to diversifying an investment portfolio to mitigate risk, diversifying income sources protects against economic uncertainties, job instability, and unexpected financial challenges.

BASIC PRINCIPLES FOR CREATING MULTIPLE INCOME STREAMS

Strategic planning

Strategic planning is essential for creating multiple revenue streams. This involves assessing skills, interests and market opportunities, setting financial goals and developing a roadmap for diversifying income sources.

Skill development

Learning various skills is essential. Whether by honing existing talents, learning new skills, or leveraging their unique strengths, individuals can improve their market value and create income opportunities in various fields.

Risk management

Creating multiple revenue streams requires a thoughtful approach to risk management. Assessing the risks associated with each revenue source and implementing strategies to mitigate potential challenges contributes to a resilient financial strategy.

Adaptability

The ability to adapt to changing circumstances is crucial. Markets evolve, industries change and technology advances – being adaptable allows individuals to identify emerging opportunities and adjust their income streams accordingly.

IMPLEMENT MULTIPLE SOURCES OF INCOME IN DAILY LIFE

Side jobs and self-employment

Engaging in side hustles or freelancing offers an immediate opportunity for additional income. This could include consulting, freelance work in your area of expertise, or passion projects with income potential.

Investments

A common approach is to invest in various assets, such as stocks, real estate or companies. Investment diversification contributes to passive income and capital appreciation, thereby ensuring long-term financial stability.

Passive income

Creating passive income streams is a key aspect. This may include dividends from investments, royalties from intellectual property, rental income, or income generated from automated online activities.

Entrepreneurship

Starting and growing a business is an important way to create additional income streams. Entrepreneurship allows people to leverage their creativity, skills and market knowledge to generate income independently.

THE TRANSFORMATIVE IMPACT OF MULTIPLE SOURCES OF INCOME

Financial resilience

One of the main benefits is greater financial resilience. Relying on a single source of income can be risky; Multiple streams act as a financial safety net, providing stability in the event of an economic crisis or unexpected life events.

Accelerated wealth creation

Creating multiple income streams accelerates wealth creation potential. Additional income streams contribute to saving, investing and debt reduction, encouraging a faster path to financial goals.

More flexibility and freedom

Diversifying income sources often leads to greater flexibility and freedom. With diverse sources of income, people can have more control over their schedule, career choices, and lifestyle.

STRATEGIES FOR CULTIVATING AND MAINTAINING MULTIPLE STREAMS OF INCOME

Management of time

Effective time management is crucial. Balancing multiple revenue streams requires strategic allocation of time and energy, ensuring each source receives the attention necessary for growth and sustainability.

Continuous learning

Staying open to continuous learning is a strategy for success. Industries evolve, skills become obsolete, and market trends change – staying informed and adaptable is essential to maintaining multiple streams of income.

Networks and collaboration

Building a strong professional network and exploring collaboration opportunities can generate new sources of income. Partnerships, joint ventures and networking provide exposure to various opportunities.

Taking advantage of technology

The use of technology is decisive. Whether it is online business, remote work, or automated investment platforms, technology can improve efficiency and expand the scope of income-generating activities.

OVERCOME THE CHALLENGES OF CREATING MULTIPLE STREAMS OF INCOME

Balance of priorities

It can be difficult to balance multiple sources of income with other life priorities. Effective prioritization, time management, and occasional reassessment of goals help maintain balance.

Investment and initial effort

Many income streams may require an initial investment, whether in terms of time, money, or effort. To meet this challenge it is necessary to understand the long-term benefits and commit to the necessary initial investment.

Risk management

Each income stream carries its own set of risks. Risk mitigation involves extensive research, diversification, and implementation of risk management strategies specific to each income source.

APPLY MULTIPLE STREAMS OF INCOME IN AREAS OF LIFE

Personal finances

Diversifying income sources improves personal finances by providing additional sources of income to spend, invest, and save. This financial stability contributes to general well-being.

Career development

Creating multiple streams of income complements traditional career paths. Side jobs, self-employment or entrepreneurial initiatives can align with career development, providing new skills and opportunities.

Retirement planning

Diversifying income sources is crucial for retirement planning. Passive income, investments and other sources can complement traditional retirement funds, providing a more comfortable and secure retirement.

THE ROLE OF MULTIPLE SOURCES OF INCOME IN ECONOMIC EMPOWERMENT

Economic independence

Creating multiple streams of income promotes financial independence. People with diverse sources of income are less dependent on a single employer or economic sector, allowing them to navigate economic changes with confidence.

Adaptability to the labor market

Having multiple sources of income improves adaptability to the labor market. This allows people to adapt and explore new opportunities, making them more resilient to industry changes or labor market fluctuations.

Entrepreneurship and Innovation

Entrepreneurship, which often contributes to the creation of multiple streams of income, contributes to economic innovation. Entrepreneurs drive economic growth by introducing new products, services and business models.

THE LIFELONG JOURNEY TO CREATING MULTIPLE STREAMS OF INCOME

Scalable income strategies

Income strategies evolve with life stages and changing goals. As people advance in their careers, personal lives and financial aspirations, the nature of their income streams can adapt to align with new goals.

Mentoring and guidance

Seeking mentorship and guidance is valuable along the way. Learning from those who have successfully created multiple streams of income can provide insights, strategies, and inspiration for lasting success.

Legacy and impact

The impact of creating multiple streams of income goes beyond individual success. Building a legacy of financial knowledge, independence and empowerment leaves a lasting impact on future generations.

In short, creating multiple streams of income is not only a financial strategy but also a transformative journey toward financial freedom and resilience. By taking a diversified approach to income generation, people are empowered to navigate economic uncertainties, pursue their passions, and achieve their financial goals with confidence.

CHAPTER SEVEN

PERSONAL GROWTH

Personal growth, often referred to as self-development, is a lifelong process of personal improvement, self-discovery and continuous learning that aims to improve various aspects of an individual's life. It involves intentional efforts to develop and expand skills, knowledge, mindset, and emotional well-being. Personal growth is a holistic journey that encompasses multiple dimensions, including intellectual, emotional, social, spiritual and physical.

Key elements and characteristics of personal growth include:

1. **Self-awareness:** Personal growth begins with self-awareness: the ability to reflect on one's thoughts, emotions, behaviors and motivations. Understanding yourself is a fundamental step in the journey towards personal development.

2. **Lifelong learning:** Personal growth involves a commitment to lifelong learning. This can take a variety of forms, including formal education, independent learning,

reading, attending workshops, and seeking new experiences to expand one's knowledge and skills.

3. **Emotional Intelligence:** Developing emotional intelligence is crucial for personal growth. This involves understanding and managing one's own emotions, feeling empathy for others, and managing social relationships effectively.

4. **Setting and Achieving Goals:** Personal growth often involves setting and pursuing meaningful goals. These goals may be related to career advancement, health and wellness, relationships, or other aspects of life. Achieving these goals contributes to a feeling of accomplishment and progress.

5. **Adaptability and Resilience:** Accepting change and developing resilience in the face of challenges are integral to personal growth. People who actively work to adapt to new circumstances and recover from setbacks foster a growth mindset.

6. **Develop healthy habits:** Cultivating positive habits, such as regular exercise, healthy eating and getting enough sleep, contributes to physical and mental well-being.

Healthy habits support overall personal growth and development.

7. **Improve Communication Skills:** Effective communication is an essential aspect of personal growth. Developing strong communication skills, including active listening, expressing thoughts clearly, and encouraging constructive dialogue, improves interpersonal relationships.

8. **Cultivate a growth mindset:** A growth mindset involves believing in your ability to learn and improve. Overcoming challenges, persisting in the face of setbacks, and viewing effort as a path to mastery are key principles of a growth mindset.

9. **Self-reflection:** Regular self-reflection is the cornerstone of personal growth. Taking the time to evaluate your values, goals and progress promotes self-awareness and allows you to adjust your behavior and state of mind.

10. **Spiritual Development:** For some people, personal growth includes spiritual or existential exploration. This might involve connecting to a higher purpose, engaging in mindfulness practices, or exploring philosophical and existential questions.

11. **Contribute to others:** Engaging in acts of kindness, volunteering, and contributing to the well-being of others is a dimension of personal growth. Helping others can give a feeling of purpose and fulfillment.

12. **Work-life balance:** Finding a balance between work responsibilities and personal life is essential to overall well-being. Personal growth involves recognizing and addressing the different dimensions of life in order to maintain a healthy balance.

Personal growth is a unique and individualized journey. It is not a destination but a continuous process of self-discovery and improvement. People embark on this journey for a variety of reasons, such as seeking fulfillment, maximizing their potential, overcoming challenges, or adapting to changing life circumstances. The pursuit of personal growth is a conscious, intentional effort to live a more meaningful, purposeful, and fulfilling life.

CONTINUOUS LEARNING: UNLEASING THE POWER OF CONTINUOUS GROWTH

In the ever-changing landscape of personal and professional development, the concept of lifelong learning is the cornerstone to unlocking people's full potential. By adopting a mindset of continuing education, adaptation and exploration, lifelong learning transcends traditional notions of formal education and becomes a dynamic and integral part of a fulfilling life journey.

UNDERSTAND CONTINUOUS LEARNING

Lifelong learning is the intentional and continuous process of acquiring new knowledge, skills, ideas and experiences throughout life. It is a mindset that encompasses curiosity, adaptability, and commitment to personal and professional development. Unlike formal education, lifelong learning extends beyond structured programs and encompasses diverse paths to acquiring wisdom.

Philosophy of permanent growth

At its core, lifelong learning embodies a philosophy of lifelong growth. It challenges the idea that education has a limited purpose, encouraging people to see every experience, challenge and encounter as an opportunity for learning and personal enrichment.

FUNDAMENTAL PRINCIPLES OF CONTINUOUS LEARNING

Curiosity and open-mindedness

Lifelong learners demonstrate a natural curiosity and open mind. They approach new ideas, perspectives and experiences with wonder, recognizing that everyone has the potential to expand their understanding of the world.

Adaptability

Adaptability is a fundamental principle of lifelong learning. In a rapidly changing world, people committed to lifelong growth remain flexible and willing to adapt their skills, strategies and perspectives to meet ever-changing challenges.

Independent learning

Continuous learning often involves self-directed initiatives. People take proactive steps to identify their areas of interest, set learning goals, and seek resources or experiences that contribute to their personal and professional development.

Knowledge integration

Lifelong learners recognize the interdependence of knowledge. They strive to integrate new information with existing understanding, creating a coherent and evolving mental framework that enriches their overall understanding of the world.

IMPLEMENTATION OF CONTINUOUS LEARNING IN DAILY LIFE

Formal education and professional development

Although lifelong learning extends beyond formal education, it often involves participation in structured programs, courses, and workshops. Earning advanced degrees, certifications, or participating in professional development opportunities are common paths.

Reading and informal learning

Reading is a powerful tool for lifelong learning. Beyond books, people use various forms of media, podcasts, online articles, and documentaries to stay informed and broaden their perspectives informally.

Skill development

Continuing education is closely linked to skills development. People actively seek opportunities to improve their existing skills or learn new ones, whether through practical experience, online tutorials or mentoring.

Networks and collaboration

Engaging with a diverse network of people is a valuable aspect of lifelong learning. Networking and collaboration expose people to different perspectives, ideas and experiences, fostering a rich environment for personal growth.

THE TRANSFORMATIVE IMPACT OF CONTINUOUS LEARNING

Career development

Continuing education contributes to professional advancement. Learning new skills and keeping up to date with industry trends improves employability, opens doors to new opportunities and positions people to advance their careers.

Intellectual stimulation

Engaging in lifelong learning provides ongoing intellectual stimulation. It keeps the mind active, promotes the feeling of curiosity and prevents stagnation, thus contributing to cognitive well-being.

Personal achievement

Lifelong learners often find personal fulfillment in the pursuit of knowledge and personal growth. The feeling of accomplishment that comes from learning new skills or understanding complex concepts adds depth and meaning to life.

STRATEGIES TO CULTIVATE AND MAINTAIN CONTINUOUS LEARNING

Define aims

Setting specific learning goals provides direction and motivation. Lifelong learners identify their areas of interest, set goals, and create a roadmap for their continued educational journey.

Management of time

Effective time management is crucial to maintaining continuous learning. People dedicate time to learning activities, prioritize their educational activities, and find balance with other life commitments.

Reflective practice

Reflective practice involves periodically evaluating one's own learning experiences. Lifelong learners reflect on their progress, identify areas for improvement, and adjust their learning strategies accordingly.

Accept challenges

Continuous learners accept challenges as opportunities for growth. They approach difficult tasks with a positive mindset, recognizing that overcoming obstacles improves resilience and deepens their understanding.

OVERCOME THE CHALLENGES OF CONTINUOUS LEARNING

Overcoming Complacency

Complacency can hinder continued learning. Meeting this challenge involves cultivating a growth mindset, seeking new challenges, and recognizing that there is always room for improvement.

Managing overrun

The abundance of information and learning options can be overwhelming. Effective lifelong learners develop the ability to set priorities, focus on high-impact learning activities, and avoid information overload.

Balance depth and width

Finding a balance between depth and breadth of knowledge is a challenge. Lifelong learners navigate through it, exploring a variety of topics while delving deeper into areas of particular interest or relevance to their goals.

APPLY CONTINUOUS LEARNING IN ALL AREAS OF LIFE

Personal growth

Continuous learning is synonymous with personal growth. Whether exploring new hobbies, learning life skills, or immersing themselves in self-help literature, people apply lifelong learning to enrich diverse aspects of their personal lives.

Family and relationships

In relationships, lifelong learning involves developing effective communication skills, understanding diverse perspectives, and seeking ideas on how to foster healthy relationships with others.

Community involvement

Engaging in the community provides ongoing students with the opportunity to understand social issues, contribute to positive change, and learn from the experiences and perspectives of others.

THE ROLE OF CONTINUOUS LEARNING IN SOCIAL DEVELOPMENT

Innovation and progress

Continuing education is a driving force for innovation and social progress. Societies that prioritize education, research, and a culture of curiosity are more likely to advance technologically, economically, and culturally.

Continuing education policies

Supportive policies that encourage lifelong learning contribute to social well-being. Governments, institutions and organizations play a role in promoting a culture of lifelong learning through accessible education and training opportunities.

Global Connectivity

In an interconnected world, lifelong learning is essential for global citizenship. Understanding diverse cultures, global issues and collaborating across borders are aspects of lifelong learning that contribute to global connectivity.

THE CONTINUOUS JOURNEY OF CONTINUOUS LEARNING

Evolving interests and passions

Continuous learning involves adapting to changing interests and passions. As people progress in life, their learning journey can lead them into new areas of fascination, causing a change in focus.

Mentoring and knowledge transfer

Mentoring and knowledge transfer are valuable elements of the lifelong learning journey. Experienced people share their knowledge and experience, fostering the growth of those looking to learn and develop.

Leave a legacy of learning

The impact of lifelong learning extends beyond individual growth. Those who engage in lifelong learning leave a legacy that inspires others to adopt a culture of curiosity, adaptability and the pursuit of knowledge.

In short, lifelong learning is not just a concept but a dynamic and transformative journey that takes place throughout life. By embracing the philosophy of lifelong growth, people become the architects of their destiny, navigating infinite horizons of knowledge, skills and personal development with passion and determination.

EXPAND YOUR SKILL SET

Expanding your skill set involves the intentional and systematic acquisition of new skills, knowledge, and abilities relevant to your personal, professional, or academic pursuits. It is a proactive approach towards self-improvement and adaptability, recognizing that the skill requirements of various fields and industries are constantly changing.

Lifelong learning mindset

At its core, expanding your skills involves a lifelong learning mindset. This goes beyond the acquisition of qualifications or degrees, and emphasizes the continuous pursuit of knowledge and the development of practical skills that align with personal and professional goals.

FUNDAMENTAL PRINCIPLES TO EXPAND YOUR SKILLS

Relevance to objectives

An effective skills expansion strategy begins with a clear understanding of personal and professional goals. People identify skills that match their aspirations, ensuring that their efforts contribute significantly to desired outcomes.

Proactive adaptation

Expanding capabilities is closely linked to proactive adaptation. Recognizing the dynamic nature of industries and professions, people are actively seeking to acquire skills that will allow them to thrive in a changing landscape.

Integration into practice

Expanding your skills is not just about theoretical knowledge; It involves the practical application of acquired skills. Successful skill expansion integrates new capabilities into daily practices, promoting mastery and efficiency.

IMPLEMENT SKILL EXPANSION IN DAILY LIFE

Formal education and training

Formal education and training programs are traditional means of acquiring skills. People complete courses, workshops, certifications and diplomas to gain structured knowledge and experience in specific areas.

Online learning platforms

The digital age has opened the door to a host of online learning opportunities. Platforms that offer various courses and tutorials allow people to learn new skills at their own pace, often from the comfort of their home.

Learning at work

Participating in on-the-job training involves learning skills through hands-on experience. People actively seek opportunities to take on new responsibilities, collaborate with colleagues, and learn from hands-on experiences.

Mentoring and networking

Mentoring and networking play a central role in broadening skills. Connecting with experienced professionals and mentors provides access to valuable information, advice, and skill-building opportunities.

THE TRANSFORMATIVE IMPACT OF SKILL EXPANSION

Career development

One of the biggest benefits of skill expansion is career advancement. Acquiring new skills improves employability, opens doors to promotions, and positions people as valuable assets in their respective fields.

Improved troubleshooting

Expanding your skills helps improve your problem-solving skills. Diverse skills give people a broader perspective, allowing them to approach challenges with creativity and a variety of solutions.

Greater confidence

As individuals master new skills, they gain greater confidence in their abilities. This increase in self-confidence positively influences decision making, leadership and achieving ambitious goals.

STRATEGIES TO CULTIVATE AND MAINTAIN SKILL EXPANSION

Self appraisal

Conducting regular self-assessments helps people identify gaps in their skills. This introspective process guides the strategic selection of the skills to acquire, ensuring alignment with personal and professional objectives.

Define aims

Setting clear, measurable goals for skills expansion provides direction and motivation. Individuals define specific skills to be acquired, as well as deadlines and milestones, encouraging a structured and intentional approach.

A consistent practice

Skill acquisition is an iterative process that requires constant practice. Regular participation in activities that reinforce newly acquired skills improves retention and mastery.

Comments and reflection

Soliciting feedback from peers, mentors, or colleagues is a valuable strategy. Constructive input provides insight into areas for improvement, guiding people to refine and perfect their skills.

OVERCOME CHALLENGES RELATED TO EXPANSION OF SKILLS

Management of time

Time constraints can pose challenges to skill development. Effective time management involves prioritizing learning activities, allocating dedicated time for skill development, and integrating learning into daily routines.

Fear of failing

Fear of failure can be a barrier to learning new skills. Meeting this challenge requires adopting a growth mindset, viewing failures as learning opportunities, and recognizing that mastery is a journey.

Balance depth and width

Finding a balance between depth and breadth of skills is essential. People address this challenge by selecting a mix of specialized skills that match their goals while maintaining a broad range of foundational knowledge.

APPLY EXPANSION OF SKILL SET IN ALL AREAS OF LIFE

Career development

In the professional field, broadening one's skills is an integral part of professional development. Acquiring skills that align with industry trends and demands enables individuals to succeed, grow and be adaptable.

Personal enrichment

Expanding your skills extends to personal enrichment. Learning new skills, whether in the creative arts, languages or hobbies, contributes to personal growth, satisfaction and a well-balanced life.

Leadership and collaboration

Effective leaders actively seek to expand their skills. Leadership skills, communication and collaboration techniques are continually honed, improving the ability to lead and inspire others.

THE ROLE OF SKILLS EXPANSION IN SOCIAL DEVELOPMENT

Innovation and progress

At the societal level, the expansion of skills stimulates innovation and progress. A population with diverse skills contributes to economic development, technological advancements and the general well-being of communities.

Lifelong learning policies

Social development benefits from policies that encourage lifelong learning. Governments and institutions play a role in creating environments that facilitate access to education, training and lifelong skills development.

Knowledge sharing

Expanding the skill set fosters a culture of knowledge sharing. People who learn new skills often become educators and mentors, passing on their experience to others and contributing to the collective knowledge base.

THE LIFETIME JOURNEY OF SKILLSET EXPANSION

Evolving Industry Trends

Expanding your skills means adapting to changing industry trends. People stay tuned to changes in their respective fields and proactively acquire skills that match emerging demands and opportunities.

Mentoring and reverse mentoring

Engaging in mentoring relationships is a lifelong practice. Individuals seek advice from experienced mentors and bring their skills and knowledge to mentoring relationships, creating a reciprocal exchange of knowledge.

Legacy of excellence

The impact of skills expansion extends beyond individual success. Those who engage in lifelong learning leave a legacy of excellence, inspiring future generations to embrace the transformative power of continued growth.

In short, developing your skills is not just a strategic effort; It is a transformative journey that shapes the trajectory of personal, professional and social development. By embracing the philosophy that skills are dynamic and adaptable, people become the architects of their destiny, shaping a dynamic future driven by a diverse and evolving skills portfolio.

CHAPTER EIGHT

NETWORK AND RELATIONSHIPS

Networking and relationships are an integral part of personal, professional, and social interactions that involve connecting with others to make meaningful connections, foster collaborations, and establish a supportive community. These two concepts are often linked but represent different dimensions of human interaction.

NETWORKS

1. **Definition:** Networking refers to the process of creating and maintaining a network of contacts, both personal and professional, in order to exchange information, resources and opportunities.

2. **Purpose:** The main objective of networking is to establish mutually beneficial connections. This may involve pursuing career opportunities, business partnerships, mentoring, or simply expanding your social circle.

3. **Methods:** Networking can be done through various channels, including professional events, social gatherings, online platforms, and industry conferences. This involves

starting conversations, exchanging contact information, and nurturing relationships over time.

4. **Skills:** Effective networking requires communication skills, interpersonal skills, and the ability to build relationships. This involves being proactive, authentic, and maintaining a positive presence in professional and social circles.

5. **Benefits:** Networking can lead to job opportunities, business collaborations, personal growth, and the exchange of valuable information. This is a strategic approach to creating a network that can provide support and open doors to new possibilities.

RELATIONS

1. **Definition:** Relationships encompass the emotional, social and personal bonds that individuals form with others. These ties can be family, romantic, friendly or professional.

2. **Purpose:** The purpose of relationships is to satisfy emotional needs, provide support, share experiences and contribute to personal well-being. Relationships are often based on trust, shared values and mutual understanding.

3. **Types:** Relationships can take many forms, including family relationships, friendships, romantic relationships, and professional relationships. Each type serves different emotional and practical purposes in an individual's life.

4. **Development:** Relationships develop over time through shared experiences, effective communication, and mutual respect. They require effort, understanding and commitment to build and maintain connections.

5. **Benefits:** Healthy relationships contribute to emotional well-being, provide a sense of belonging, and offer support in difficult and joyful times. Positive relationships improve quality of life and contribute to personal growth.

INTERCONNECTION

1. **Overlap:** Networks and relationships often overlap, especially in professional settings. Professional relationships can evolve into real relationships based on shared values, trust and mutual support.

2. **Build Trust:** Networking and relationships require building trust. Trust is the foundation of meaningful relationships, whether in a professional context or within personal circles.

3. **Long-term perspective:** Although networking may initially be motivated by specific goals or interests, maintaining long-term connections often turns these interactions into real relationships. Long-term relationships can, in turn, become valuable professional networks.

4. **Support system:** Relationships, both personal and professional, can serve as a support system at different stages of life. Networking connections can also offer support in terms of career advice, mentoring, or collaboration opportunities.

In short, networking is a deliberate and strategic effort to create a professional or social network, while relationships encompass a broader spectrum of personal and emotional connections. Both are essential for personal and professional growth, and networking often serves as a gateway to building meaningful relationships over time. The balance between these two aspects contributes to a complete and satisfying social and professional life.

BUILD A SUPPORT NETWORK

Building a support network involves intentionally creating a community of people who provide encouragement, advice, and assistance. It is a proactive effort to surround oneself with people who share common values, goals or interests and who contribute positively to personal and professional endeavors.

Aim

The main purpose of a support network is to offer emotional, practical and professional support. It serves as a safety net in difficult times, a source of inspiration and a platform for collaboration and mutual growth.

BASIC PRINCIPLES FOR BUILDING A SUPPORT NETWORK

Mutual respect and trust

Mutual respect and trust form the basis of a support network. Authentic relationships are based on transparency, trustworthiness and a true understanding of each other's strengths and challenges.

Reciprocity

Reciprocity is a key principle. Building a support network involves a give-and-take dynamic, in which individuals contribute to the well-being and success of others as much as they receive support themselves.

Diversity

A support network benefits from diversity. Including people with diverse backgrounds, perspectives and skills enriches the network and provides a variety of knowledge and resources.

STRATEGIES TO BUILD AND FOSTER A SUPPORT NETWORK

Identification of fundamental values and objectives

Clarifying personal and professional values and goals is the first step. People seek connections with those who share similar values and aspirations, fostering a sense of unity within the network.

Networking Events and Communities

Attending networking events, both in person and online, provides the opportunity to meet like-minded people. Joining communities, professional organizations or interest groups helps expand your network.

Authentic communication

Authenticity is crucial to establishing and maintaining connections. True communication involves sharing experiences, expressing vulnerabilities, and celebrating successes, thereby fostering deeper, more meaningful connections.

Offer support

Actively offering support to others within the network strengthens relationships. Whether through mentoring, collaboration or listening, contributing positively to others creates a favorable and reciprocal environment.

THE TRANSFORMATIVE IMPACT OF A SUPPORT NETWORK

Emotional well-being

A support network contributes to emotional well-being. In difficult times, having a network of supportive people brings comfort, encouragement and a feeling of belonging.

Professional growth

In the professional field, a support network facilitates professional development. Network connections provide advice, mentoring, and potential opportunities, thereby enhancing an individual's professional development.

Resilience

The collective strength of a support network improves resilience. Overcoming challenges becomes more manageable with the encouragement, advice and shared experiences that the network offers.

OVERCOME CHALLENGES BY BUILDING A SUPPORT NETWORK

Quality over quantity

Prioritizing the quality of connections over quantity is essential. Building a small, real network often has more impact than accumulating many superficial connections.

Balance reciprocity

Maintaining a balance of reciprocity can be a challenge. It is important to contribute to the network while recognizing and accepting support when needed.

Manage expectations

Realistic expectations are crucial. Building a support network takes time and not every connection will develop into a deep and meaningful relationship. Managing expectations avoids disappointment.

APPLY A SUPPORT NETWORK IN AREAS OF LIFE

Personal relationships

A support network extends to personal relationships. Friends, family, and loved ones contribute to emotional well-being by providing a foundation of support and love.

Academic activities

In academia, building a support network involves connecting with classmates, professors, and mentors. Collaborative study groups, mentoring relationships, and academic communities enhance the learning experience.

Entrepreneurship and business

Entrepreneurs benefit greatly from a support network. Relationships with mentors, fellow entrepreneurs, and professionals in related industries provide guidance, partnerships, and leads.

THE ROLE OF A SUPPORT NETWORK IN SOCIAL DEVELOPMENT

Community building

Support networks contribute to community development. People linked by shared values or common goals can collaborate on community projects, initiatives or services, thus promoting positive social development.

Mentoring programs

Implementing mentoring programs within communities and industries promotes knowledge transfer and support. Experienced people advise those in the early stages of their careers, contributing to overall social growth.

Social capital

Support networks contribute to the development of social capital within societies. Social capital, characterized by trust and cooperation, improves the overall well-being and resilience of communities.

THE JOURNEY OF A LIFETIME TO BUILD A SUPPORT NETWORK

Scalable connections

Building a support network is a dynamic process. Connections evolve over time as individuals develop personally and professionally, and the network adapts to new goals and aspirations.

Lifelong learning

Commitment to lifelong learning is closely linked to creating a support network. People continue to learn from the experiences and ideas of others within the network, fostering continued growth.

Leave a legacy of support

The impact of building a support network extends beyond individual success. Those who commit to cultivating connections leave a legacy of support, inspiring others to build and maintain networks that contribute to collective well-being.

In short, building a support network is not just a strategic effort; It is a transformative journey that shapes the trajectory of personal, professional and social development.

By intentionally cultivating connections based on trust, respect, and reciprocity, individuals become the architects of their destiny, fostering a culture of encouragement, collaboration, and shared success.

EXPLOIT CONNECTIONS

Leveraging connections is the strategic use of one's network to obtain information, resources, support and opportunities. It is about identifying and harnessing the collective strength of relationships to achieve specific goals, whether personal or professional.

Aim

The main goal of leveraging connections is to maximize the potential of the network for mutual benefit. This may include accessing information, obtaining opportunities, collaborating on projects, or advancing professionally or personally.

FUNDAMENTAL PRINCIPLES FOR THE USE OF CONNECTIONS

Reciprocity

Reciprocity remains a fundamental principle. Leveraging connections is not a one-way street; It involves a give-and-take dynamic in which individuals contribute to the success and well-being of other network members.

Trust and credibility

Trust and credibility are paramount. Effectively leveraging connections relies on a foundation of trust, where people can confidently share ideas, recommendations and opportunities within the network.

Added value

Creating value within the network is crucial. People who actively contribute to the growth and success of their relationships are more likely to find reciprocity when they seek to benefit from those relationships.

STRATEGIES FOR EFFECTIVE USE OF CONNECTION

Clear articulation of objectives

Clear articulation of objectives is essential. Individuals should identify the specific goals they intend to achieve by leveraging relationships, whether that be career advancement, business growth, or personal development.

Targeted communication

Effective communication involves clearly conveying needs, goals and intentions. Tailoring communication to the preferences and interests of each connection increases the likelihood of successful use.

Active listening

Active listening is a valuable skill. Understanding the needs and aspirations of network members allows people to offer support and resources more effectively.

Personal brand

Building a strong personal brand helps you successfully leverage connection. A positive, authentic personal brand improves credibility, making people more attractive collaborators within your network.

THE TRANSFORMATIVE IMPACT OF LEVERAGING CONNECTIONS

Career advancement

Leveraging relationships significantly contributes to career advancement. Whether you're looking for career opportunities, mentorship, or industry insights, well-utilized connections can help achieve your career goals.

Business Growth

Entrepreneurs and professionals can leverage their relationships to drive business growth. Collaborations, partnerships and access to resources within the network can boost businesses.

Knowledge expansion

The exchange of knowledge within a network is a transformative aspect. Leveraging connections for diverse learning opportunities, knowledge and perspectives contributes to ongoing personal and professional development.

OVERCOME CHALLENGES USING CONNECTIONS

Authenticity

Maintaining authenticity can be a challenge. People need to find a balance between leveraging connections for mutual benefit and ensuring that interactions remain authentic and sincere.

Balance reciprocity

Balancing reciprocity requires delicacy. If individuals seek to benefit from their network, they must also actively contribute to the success and well-being of their relationships.

Avoid overdependence

Relying too much on connections without independent efforts can be a danger. People must leverage their connections strategically while independently cultivating their skills and experience.

USE CONNECTION IN ALL AREAS OF LIFE

Career transitions

Leveraging connections during career transitions can make the process easier. Seeking advice, mentoring, and potential job opportunities within your professional network makes the transition simpler.

Business projects

Entrepreneurs can leverage connections to launch and grow their businesses. Access to potential investors, collaborators and mentors within the network can have a significant impact on the success of entrepreneurial efforts.

Personal development

In personal development, leveraging relationships means seeking advice, support, and mentoring. The network becomes a source of wisdom and encouragement in the search for personal development.

THE ROLE OF CONNECTIONS LEVER IN SOCIAL DEVELOPMENT

Collaboration and innovation

Leveraging connection contributes to collaboration and innovation within societies. People and organizations working collaboratively within their networks can generate positive social change.

Mentoring Programs

Implementing mentoring programs that encourage leveraging connections encourages the transfer of knowledge and support. Experienced people within the network advise those in need, thereby contributing to overall social growth.

Share capital

Leveraging connection improves social capital within communities. Trust and cooperation developed through strategic connections have a positive impact on social well-being.

THE LIFETIME JOURNEY TO USING CONNECTIONS

Evolving relationships

Leveraging connections is a dynamic process. Relationships within the network evolve over time, adapting to changing goals, aspirations, and life stages.

Lifelong learning

A commitment to lifelong learning is critical to leveraging connections effectively. People continue to learn from the experiences and ideas of others within the network, fostering continued growth.

Leave a legacy of collaboration

The impact of leveraging connections extends beyond individual success. Those who engage in strategic relationships leave a legacy of collaboration, inspiring others to harness the power of their networks to achieve collective achievements.

In short, leveraging connections is not just a skill; is a transformational strategy that enables people to unlock opportunities, achieve their goals and navigate the complexities of an interconnected world. By intentionally cultivating and strategically using their networks, people become the architects of their destiny, fostering a culture of collaboration, growth, and shared success.

CHAPTER NINE

THE ENTERPRISE SPIRIT

Entrepreneurship refers to a set of characteristics, attitudes and mindsets associated with entrepreneurs, that is, innovative, risk-taking people committed to creating, developing and managing new businesses. This spirit encompasses a variety of qualities that enable people to identify opportunities, take calculated risks, and pursue their vision with determination and resilience. These are the key elements that define the entrepreneurial spirit:

1. Innovation and creativity

• Entrepreneurs are known for their ability to think creatively and find innovative solutions to problems. They often challenge the status quo and look for new ways to meet market needs or improve existing products and services.

2. Risk assumption

• Entrepreneurship involves the willingness to take calculated risks. Entrepreneurs understand that uncertainty and risk are inherent in business and are often comfortable stepping out of their comfort zone to pursue opportunities.

3. Vision and ambition

• Entrepreneurs have a clear vision of what they want to achieve and the ambition to tirelessly pursue their goals. They set long-term goals and work strategically to achieve their aspirations.

4. Initiative and proactivity

• Entrepreneurs are proactive people who take the initiative to turn their ideas into actions. They do not wait for opportunities to be presented to them, but actively seek and create them themselves.

5. Adaptability

• An entrepreneurial mindset involves being adaptable and responsive to changing circumstances. Entrepreneurs understand the dynamic nature of business and are willing to develop their strategies as necessary.

6. Persistence and Resilience

• Building and growing a business is often challenging and setbacks are inevitable. Entrepreneurs demonstrate perseverance and resilience, recover from failures, and learn from their experiences to overcome obstacles.

7. Ingenuity

• Entrepreneurs are resourceful people who can make the most of limited resources. They find creative solutions, leverage networks, and maximize available assets to achieve their goals.

8. Customer-centric approach

• Successful entrepreneurs prioritize understanding customer needs and providing value to their target audience. They are customer-focused and often seek feedback to improve products or services.

9. Leadership and Decision Making

• Entrepreneurs are natural leaders who can make decisions under conditions of uncertainty. They take responsibility for their businesses, guide their teams, and make informed decisions that align with their vision.

10. Passion and enthusiasm

• Passion is the driving force behind entrepreneurship. Entrepreneurs have a deep passion for their ideas and projects, which fuels their dedication, perseverance and commitment to success.

11. Networking and Relationship Building

• Entrepreneurs understand the importance of creating and leveraging networks. They actively seek relationships, collaborate with others, and recognize the value of relationships in business development.

12. Continuous Learning

• An entrepreneurial spirit involves a commitment to learning and continuous improvement. Entrepreneurs stay informed about industry trends, seek knowledge, and adapt to changing market conditions.

Ultimately, entrepreneurship is a dynamic, multi-faceted mindset that drives people to create, innovate, and contribute to the growth and development of businesses and economies.

UNLEASH CREATIVITY

Creativity is the process of making something new, original and valuable a reality. It covers a range of activities, from artistic expression and scientific innovation to problem solving and entrepreneurial initiatives.

Inherent human capacity

Creativity is an inherent human ability that manifests itself in various ways. This is not limited to artistic pursuits but extends to all aspects of life, including business, science, technology and everyday problem solving.

FUNDAMENTAL PRINCIPLES FOR DEVELOPING CREATIVITY

Open mind

Open-mindedness is essential to creativity. People must be willing to explore new ideas, perspectives and possibilities without preconceived notions, allowing their minds to wander freely.

Curiosity

Curiosity is the engine of creativity. A natural propensity to ask questions, seek to understand and explore the unknown fuels the creative process.

Intrepidity

Creativity often involves taking risks and venturing into the unknown. Courage is a key principle that allows people to overcome fear of failure and accept uncertainty as part of the creative journey.

STRATEGIES TO UNLEASH CREATIVITY

Cultivate a creative environment

Creating an environment that encourages creativity is essential. This means providing space for experimentation, encouraging collaboration and removing barriers that stifle innovation.

Adopt diverse perspectives

Diversity of thought and perspective is a catalyst for creativity. Interacting with people from different backgrounds, experiences and disciplines provides a wealth of ideas that generate innovation.

Accept failure as a learning opportunity

Failure is an integral part of the creative process. Accepting failure as a valuable learning opportunity allows people to iterate, refine, and ultimately improve their creative pursuits.

Mindfulness and reflection

Mindfulness practices, such as meditation and reflection, help unlock creativity. These practices promote a clear and focused mind, allowing for deeper exploration of ideas and knowledge.

THE TRANSFORMATIVE IMPACT OF THE LIBERATION OF CREATIVITY

Innovation and problem solving

Unleashing creativity drives innovation and problem solving. Creative thinking allows individuals to approach challenges with new perspectives, leading to new solutions and breakthroughs.

Personal growth and development

Creativity is a path to growth and personal fulfillment. Engaging in creative activities provides a sense of purpose, self-expression and a way to explore one's identity.

Improved communication

Creativity improves communication by allowing people to express their ideas in unique and compelling ways.

Creative communication resonates with audiences, fostering connection and understanding.

OVERCOME CHALLENGES TO UNLEASH CREATIVITY

Overcoming Self-Doubt

Self-doubt can be a major barrier to creativity. Meeting this challenge involves cultivating trust, accepting imperfection, and recognizing that creativity is a process of continuous improvement.

Break the routine

Creativity often flourishes outside of routine. Breaking established patterns and exploring new experiences stimulates new ideas and perspectives.

Dealing with fear of judgment

Fear of judgment can stifle creativity. Facing this challenge involves creating a safe space for exploration, valuing process over perfection, and embracing vulnerability.

APPLY CREATIVITY IN ALL AREAS OF LIFE

Professional settings

Unleashing creativity in the workplace improves problem solving, encourages innovation, and contributes to a culture of continuous improvement. Creative thinking is a valuable asset when facing complex challenges.

Education and learning

Promoting creativity in education encourages students to think critically, explore diverse perspectives, and engage in active, hands-on learning experiences. Creative teaching methods enhance the learning journey.

Personal development

Creativity plays an essential role in personal development. Engaging in creative activities, whether through the arts, writing, or other forms of expression, contributes to self-discovery, emotional well-being, and a sense of fulfillment.

THE ROLE OF DEVELOPING CREATIVITY IN SOCIAL DEVELOPMENT

Cultural enrichment

Creativity enriches culture by contributing to artistic expressions, literature, and the creation of shared narratives. It shapes the identity of societies and fosters a sense of collective imagination.

Technological advances

Technological progress is often driven by creative thinking. Innovations in science, engineering and technology arise from the imaginative exploration of possibilities.

Social change and promotion

Creative approaches are powerful tools for social change and advocacy. Creative campaigns, art and storytelling can raise awareness, challenge norms and inspire collective action.

THE JOURNEY OF A LIFETIME TO RELEASE CREATIVITY

Embrace continuous learning

Creativity is a journey of lifelong learning. Embracing new ideas, staying curious, and evolving with a changing landscape all contribute to sustained creative growth.

Mentoring and collaboration

Engaging in mentoring and collaboration promotes the exchange of ideas and knowledge, contributing to the continued development of creative thinking.

Leave a Legacy of Creative Expression

The impact of unleashing creativity extends beyond individual activities. Those who engage in creative expression leave a legacy of inspiration, shaping the cultural and intellectual landscape for future generations.

In short, unlocking creativity is not simply a process but a dynamic and transformative journey that unfolds throughout life. By having an open mind, cultivating diverse perspectives, and overcoming challenges, individuals become the architects of their creative destiny, navigating infinite horizons of innovation, expression, and fulfillment.

TAKE CALCULATED RISKS

Calculated risk-taking refers to the process of making decisions that involve uncertainties and potential outcomes, with careful consideration of potential benefits and harms. It is a strategic approach that seeks to maximize opportunities while minimizing potential negative consequences.

Inherent nature of risk

Risk is an inherent aspect of life and progress. Taking calculated risks recognizes that growth often involves stepping out of your comfort zone, exploring uncharted territories, and embracing the unknown.

FUNDAMENTAL PRINCIPLES OF CALCULATED RISK TAKING

Informed decision making

Taking calculated risks depends on informed decision making. This involves gathering relevant information, conducting a thorough analysis, and evaluating potential outcomes before making a decision.

Risk tolerance

Understanding your risk tolerance is crucial. This involves recognizing the level of uncertainty and discomfort one is willing to endure in pursuit of a goal or opportunity.

Balance of possible gains and losses

A key principle is the art of balancing potential gains and losses. Strategic decision-making considers not only potential rewards, but also potential setbacks and their impact.

CALCULATED RISK-TAKING STRATEGIES

Set clear goals

Clearly defining objectives is essential. Knowing what you intend to achieve provides a framework for assessing whether the potential benefits outweigh the risks.

Perform a risk analysis

A thorough analysis of potential risks involves assessing their likelihood, their potential impact, and the organization's or individual's ability to effectively manage or mitigate them.

Diversification

Risk diversification involves spreading investments, efforts or initiatives through different channels. This strategy minimizes the impact of a negative result in one area on the overall situation.

Establish contingency plans

Developing contingency plans is a proactive approach to risk management. Having a plan in place to deal with potential setbacks improves preparation and resilience.

THE TRANSFORMATIVE IMPACT OF CALCULATED RISK-TAKING

Innovation and growth

Taking calculated risks is a catalyst for innovation and growth. This opens doors to new ideas, businesses and opportunities that can propel people and organizations forward.

Learning and adaptation

The process of taking calculated risks fosters a culture of continuous learning and adaptation. Setbacks become opportunities for reflection and improvement, contributing to continued development.

Greater confidence

Successfully managing calculated risks builds confidence. Each strategic decision becomes a springboard that affirms its ability to take on challenges and make informed decisions.

OVERCOME CHALLENGES BY TAKING CALCULATED RISKS

Fear of failing

Fear of failure can be a major obstacle. Meeting this challenge requires viewing failure as a valuable learning experience and recognizing that it is an integral part of taking risks.

Paralysis from overanalysis:

Excessive analysis of potential risks can lead to indecision. Finding the balance between careful analysis and decisive action is crucial for effective risk taking.

Lack of flexibility

Rigidity can hinder the ability to adapt to unexpected outcomes. Embracing flexibility allows people and organizations to respond to changing circumstances with agility.

APPLY RISK-TAKING IN ALL AREAS OF LIFE

Career advancement

In the professional field, taking calculated risks is essential to advance in your career. This means pursuing ambitious projects, seeking new opportunities, and standing up for yourself.

Entrepreneurship

Entrepreneurs thrive by taking calculated risks. Starting a business, introducing new products or entering new markets requires a strategic approach to risk-taking.

Personal development

On a personal level, taking calculated risks contributes to personal development. This may involve pursuing further education, exploring new hobbies or changing your lifestyle.

THE ROLE OF CALCULATED RISK-TAKING IN SOCIAL DEVELOPMENT

Economic progress

Social progress often depends on economic development, which, in turn, involves calculated risk-taking by businesses, investors and policymakers to drive innovation and growth.

Scientific and technological advances

Scientific and technological advancements are driven by researchers and innovators who take calculated risks by exploring uncharted territories and pushing the boundaries of knowledge.

Social innovation

Addressing social challenges and fostering social innovation requires the courage to take calculated risks when developing and implementing new solutions and initiatives.

THE LIFE JOURNEY TO TAKE CALCULATED RISKS

Adaptation and evolution

Taking calculated risks is a lifelong journey of adaptation and evolution. As circumstances change, individuals and organizations must continually evaluate and adjust their risk management strategies.

Mentoring and Guidance

Participating in mentoring and seeking advice from experienced people can provide valuable information and perspectives on effective risk taking.

Leave a Legacy of Bold Decision Making

The impact of taking calculated risks extends beyond individual success. Those who participate in strategic decision-making leave a legacy of boldness, inspiring others to face uncertainty with courage and determination.

In short, taking calculated risks is not just a gamble, but an art of deliberate and strategic decision-making that shapes the trajectory of personal, professional and social development. By adopting informed decision-making, balancing potential gains and losses, and learning from their experiences, people become the architects of their destiny and navigate uncertainty with determination and courage.

CHAPTER TEN

HEALTH AND WELLNESS

Health and well-being refers to the general state of physical, mental and social health of an individual. It goes beyond the absence of disease and encompasses a holistic approach to achieving and maintaining a high quality of life. a person.

COMPONENTS OF HEALTH AND WELL-BEING

1. Physical Health:

• Physical health involves the proper functioning of the body and its organs. This includes factors such as nutrition, exercise, sleep, and freedom from illness. Regular physical activity, a balanced diet and sufficient rest are essential elements of physical well-being.

2. Mental Health:

• Mental well-being encompasses emotional and psychological health. It involves the ability to cope with stress, maintain positive relationships, and manage life's challenges effectively. Mental health includes emotional resilience, self-esteem, and the ability to approach various aspects of life with a positive mindset.

3. Social Health:

• Social health refers to the quality of an individual's social relationships and connections. Strong social support, meaningful connections with others, and a sense of belonging contribute to social well-being. Positive social interactions can improve emotional and mental health.

4. Emotional well-being:

• Emotional well-being involves understanding and effectively managing your emotions. This includes the ability to express emotions appropriately, cope with stress, and maintain a sense of balance and resilience in the face of life's ups and downs.

5. Spiritual Health:

• Spiritual well-being is linked to a sense of purpose, meaning, and connection to something larger than oneself. It may involve personal beliefs, values, or a connection to a higher power. Spiritual health contributes to a sense of fulfillment and purpose in life.

6. Environmental factors:

• The environment in which a person lives and works can affect their health and well-being. Access to clean air, water, and a safe living environment are essential for physical health. Additionally, factors such as job satisfaction and work-life balance play a role in overall well-being.

IMPORTANCE OF HEALTH AND WELL-BEING

1. Quality of life:

• Health and well-being contribute significantly to an individual's overall quality of life. A healthy person is better able to enjoy life, pursue personal goals, and participate in meaningful activities.

2. Productivity and performance:

• People who prioritize health and well-being often experience greater productivity and performance in various aspects of life, including work, relationships, and personal activities.

3. Disease Prevention:

• The focus on health and wellness includes preventative measures to avoid illness and maintain optimal physical and mental health. Regular exercise, a balanced diet and stress control can help prevent disease.

4. Resilience in the face of challenges:

• Those who enjoy good health and well-being tend to be more resilient in the face of life's challenges. They are better equipped to cope with stress, adapt to change and recover from setbacks.

5. Positive relationships:

• Health and social well-being are closely linked to positive relationships. People with strong social connections tend to experience greater emotional support, reduced feelings of loneliness, and greater overall well-being.

6. Longevity:

• Research suggests that a healthy lifestyle and general well-being are associated with longer life expectancy. Adopting healthy habits can contribute to a longer, more fulfilled life.

PROMOTE HEALTH AND WELL-BEING

1. Balanced diet:

• A nutritious, balanced diet is essential for physical health because it provides the body with the nutrients it needs to function optimally.

2. Regular exercise:

• Physical activity contributes to physical and mental well-being. Regular exercise promotes cardiovascular health, strengthens muscles and improves mood.

3. Sufficient sleep:

• Quality sleep is crucial for overall health. It allows the body to rest and recover, thus promoting physical and mental well-being.

4. Stress management:

• Effective stress management techniques, such as mindfulness, meditation and relaxation exercises, contribute to mental and emotional well-being.

5. Social Connections:

• Establishing and maintaining positive relationships with friends, family, and community members improves social health and provides a support system during difficult times.

6. Mental Health Support:

• Seeking professional help when needed and prioritizing mental health screenings are essential to maintaining emotional well-being.

7. Balance between personal and professional life:

• Balancing work and personal life helps prevent burnout and promotes overall well-being. Taking breaks, setting boundaries, and prioritizing self-care all contribute to a healthier lifestyle.

8. Community participation:

• Participating in community activities and contributing to the well-being of others fosters a sense of belonging and purpose.

9. Periodic Health Checks:

• Regular health checks and examinations help detect potential health problems early, allowing for rapid intervention and preventative measures.

10. Lifelong Learning:

• Engaging in lifelong learning and personal development contributes to mental and emotional well-being, providing a sense of accomplishment and purpose.

At its core, health and wellness are dynamic, interconnected aspects of a person's life that require ongoing attention and care. By adopting a holistic approach that addresses physical, mental and social well-being, people can cultivate the foundations of a full and balanced life.

HOLISTIC PROSPERITY

Holistic prosperity is a concept that transcends traditional notions of wealth and success, emphasizing a holistic, interconnected approach to well-being and abundance. It encompasses the idea that true prosperity extends beyond financial achievements to include physical health, mental well-being, meaningful relationships, personal growth and a sense of purpose. This holistic perspective recognizes the interaction of various dimensions of life and seeks to foster a balanced and fulfilling existence. In this exploration, we delve deeper into the principles, components and transformative impact of holistic prosperity.

PRINCIPLES OF HOLISTIC PROSPERITY

1. Interconnectivity:

• Holistic prosperity recognizes the interconnected nature of the different dimensions of life. Recognize that physical health, mental well-being, relationships and overall fulfillment are closely linked.

2. Balance and Harmony:

• Achieving comprehensive prosperity involves finding balance and harmony between the different aspects of life. It emphasizes avoiding extremes and fostering a sense of balance in the pursuit of well-being.

3. Live consciously:

• Mindfulness is a key principle of holistic prosperity. It involves being present in the moment, making conscious decisions, and cultivating awareness of one's thoughts, actions, and their impact on well-being.

4. **Continued growth:**

• Holistic prosperity values continuous personal and professional growth. It encompasses a lifelong journey of learning, self-discovery and development in various areas of life.

5. **Purpose and Meaning:**

• A sense of purpose and meaning is an integral part of holistic prosperity. This involves aligning actions with values, setting meaningful goals, and thriving by contributing to something bigger than yourself.

COMPONENTS OF HOLISTIC PROSPERITY

1. **Physical well-being:**

• Holistic prosperity begins with physical health. Regular physical activity, a balanced diet, enough sleep, and preventative health care contribute to overall well-being.

2. Mental and emotional health:

• Mental and emotional well-being is essential. Holistic prosperity involves managing stress, building resilience, and cultivating a positive mindset.

3. Financial Wellbeing:

• Although it is not the only objective, financial well-being is considered part of comprehensive prosperity. It involves responsible financial management, saving and investing to support the lifestyle you want.

4. Meaningful relationships:

• Maintaining meaningful connections and relationships with family, friends, and community is an essential aspect of well-rounded prosperity. Social support contributes to emotional well-being.

5. Personal growth:

• Holistic prosperity values continuous personal growth. This includes learning new skills, expanding knowledge and taking advantage of opportunities for personal development.

6. Spiritual well-being:

• Spiritual well-being involves connecting with one's own values, beliefs and sense of purpose. This is not necessarily linked to religious practices, but rather encompasses a broader understanding of the meaning of life.

7. Harmony between work and personal life:

• Achieving harmony between personal and work life is crucial. Holistic prosperity recognizes the importance of a fulfilling career while ensuring that time and energy are also dedicated to personal interests and relationships.

8. Environmental Awareness:

• Comprehensive prosperity extends to environmental awareness. This means adopting sustainable practices, contributing to ecological well-being and recognizing the interconnectedness of humanity and the planet.

TRANSFORMATIVE IMPACT OF HOLISTIC PROSPERITY

1. Improved well-being:

• Comprehensive prosperity leads to greater general well-being. When people prioritize multiple dimensions of life, they experience greater satisfaction, joy, and a sense of fulfillment.

2. Resilience in the face of adversity:

• A holistic approach promotes resilience in the face of challenges. When people have a solid foundation of physical, mental, and emotional well-being, they are better equipped to deal with adversity.

3. Improved Relationships:

• Maintaining meaningful relationships contributes to a support system that improves emotional well-being. Holistic prosperity recognizes the importance of positive social connections to foster a sense of community.

4. Sense of purpose:

• Holistic prosperity gives people a sense of purpose and direction. Aligning actions with personal values and contributing to the well-being of others cultivates a deeper sense of meaning in life.

5. Lasting Success:

• Success is seen through the lens of sustainability. Holistic prosperity emphasizes long-term well-being rather than short-term gains, ensuring that achievements are aligned with personal values and contribute positively to life.

6. Contributions to the Company:

• Holistic prosperity encourages individuals to contribute positively to society. When people experience abundance in various aspects of life, they are more likely to engage in activities that benefit others and the community.

CULTIVATING HOLISTIC PROSPERITY

1. Personal Reflection:

• Regular self-reflection allows individuals to assess their alignment with holistic prosperity principles and identify areas for growth and improvement.

2. Set goals:

• Setting holistic goals that encompass various dimensions of life ensures a balanced and comprehensive approach to personal and professional development.

3. Mindfulness Practices:

• Engaging in mindfulness practices, such as meditation and mindfulness exercises, improves awareness and encourages a present-centered approach to life.

4. Continuous Learning:

• Adopting a mindset of continuous learning contributes to personal growth. The pursuit of education and skills development opportunities aligns with the holistic path to prosperity.

5. Environmental management:

• Adopting environmentally friendly practices contributes to overall prosperity. People can make decisions that align with sustainable living and promote ecological well-being.

6. Social commitment:

• Active participation in social and community activities promotes meaningful connections and contributes to a sense of social well-being.

In short, holistic prosperity represents a way of living that embraces abundance in various dimensions of life. By prioritizing physical health, mental well-being, meaningful relationships, personal growth and a sense of purpose, people can navigate life's journey with resilience, fulfillment and a deep appreciation of interdependence well-being. Holistic prosperity is not a destination but a lifelong journey of self-discovery, growth and positive contribution to self, others and the world.

WORK-LIFE BALANCE

In the demanding and fast-paced landscape of the modern world, achieving a harmonious work-life balance is a pursuit that is of paramount importance to personal well-being and overall fulfillment. Balancing these two spheres involves consciously navigating between professional responsibilities and personal aspirations, ensuring that neither overshadows the other.

PRINCIPLES FOR BALANCING LIFE AND WORK

1. Prioritization:

• Balancing work and life requires a keen sense of prioritization. Identifying and focusing on key priorities, both professionally and personally, is essential for effective time management.

2. Limitations:

• Setting clear boundaries is crucial. Setting limits on work hours, avoiding constant connectivity, and creating dedicated time for personal activities helps prevent burnout and encourage a healthier balance.

3. Flexibility:

• Flexibility is the cornerstone of work-life balance. Embracing adaptability allows people to cope with unexpected demands without sacrificing their personal well-being.

4. Quality over quantity:

• It is essential to emphasize the quality of time spent on work and personal activities. The search for efficiency and effectiveness guarantees that the impact of actions is significant and satisfactory.

STRATEGIES TO BALANCE LIFE AND WORK

1. Time management:

• Effective time management involves setting realistic goals, prioritizing tasks and allocating time intelligently. Using tools and techniques, such as calendars and to-do lists, helps maximize productivity.

2. Life-work integration:

• Integrating work and personal life, rather than strictly separating them, allows for a more fluid balance. This approach involves finding synergies between professional and personal goals.

3. Effective communication:

• Clear and open communication with co-workers, supervisors and family is essential. Communicating priorities and expectations ensures understanding and support from all parties.

4. Conscious Presence:

• Being present in the moment is key to work-life balance. Whether at work or with our loved ones, practicing mindfulness promotes deeper connection and enjoyment of the present.

TRANSFORMATIVE IMPACT OF WORK-LIFE BALANCE

1. Improved well-being:

• Achieving a balance between personal and work life helps improve overall well-being. People experience less stress, better mental health, and greater satisfaction in professional and personal aspects of life.

2. Greater productivity:

• Work-life balance has a positive impact on productivity. When people are well-rested, mentally refreshed, and feel fulfilled in their personal activities, their performance and effectiveness in their professional endeavors often experience significant improvement.

3. Stronger relationships:

• Maintaining personal relationships requires time and attention. Finding balance allows people to invest in and strengthen their connections with family and friends, fostering a positive and fulfilling personal life.

4. Prevention of burnout:

• A well-managed work-life balance acts as a preventive measure against burnout. Recognizing and addressing signs of excessive stress or fatigue ensures sustained engagement and enthusiasm in both areas.

5. Job satisfaction:

• People who successfully balance work and family life often report higher levels of job satisfaction. A feeling of accomplishment in personal life has a positive impact on professional achievements and vice versa.

OVERCOME CHALLENGES TO BALANCE LIFE AND WORK

1. Set clear boundaries:

• Establishing and maintaining clear boundaries between work and personal life can be difficult. It is crucial to communicate and reinforce these boundaries consistently.

2. Delegation of Responsibilities:

• Learning to delegate tasks, both at work and at home, is vital. Delegation allows people to share the workload, reducing stress and freeing up time for personal activities.

3. Time management skills:

• Developing effective time management skills is an ongoing process. This requires constant self-evaluation, adaptation and commitment to perfect organizational strategies.

APPLY WORK-LIFE BALANCE IN AREAS OF LIFE

1. Professional Growth:

• Balancing work and personal life does not hinder professional growth; On the contrary, it improves it. People can pursue their professional ambitions while promoting their well-being and personal relationships.

2. Parenting and family life:

• Finding balance is especially crucial for parents. Prioritizing family time, assuming shared responsibilities, and encouraging open communication contribute to a harmonious family life.

3. Personal development:

• Personal development and growth thrive in a balanced environment. Pursuing hobbies, education, and personal development activities outside of work enriches your personal life.

THE JOURNEY OF A LIFETIME TO BALANCE LIFE AND WORK

1. Adaptability:

• Balancing work and personal life is a dynamic process that requires adaptability. Life circumstances, work demands, and personal priorities change, requiring adjustments along the way.

2. Continuous Reflection:

• Regular self-reflection is essential to maintaining a healthy balance. Individuals should periodically evaluate their priorities, values, and goals to ensure their actions align with their desired work-life balance.

3. Accept the change:

• Embracing change is inherent to the journey of balancing work and personal life. Being open to adjusting strategies, reassessing priorities, and embracing new opportunities ensures continued growth and satisfaction.

In short, balancing work and life is a dynamic and nuanced pursuit that requires conscious effort, adaptability, and a commitment to personal well-being. By adopting principles of prioritization, setting boundaries, and implementing effective strategies, individuals can navigate work responsibilities and personal aspirations. The transformative impact is felt not only in greater well-being and productivity, but also in the cultivation of a satisfying and harmonious life that encompasses both professional and personal spheres.

CHAPTER ELEVEN

EMBRACE SUCCESS

Accepting success is the conscious and positive recognition, acceptance and celebration of one's achievements and accomplishments. It involves a mindset that recognizes and appreciates personal victories, milestones and goal achievement. Accepting success goes beyond simply achieving external indicators of success; It encompasses an internal and subjective recognition of one's own growth, efforts and achievement of one's aspirations.

Key aspects for success:

1. Recognition:

• Accepting success begins with recognizing and acknowledging your own achievements. This involves consciously taking stock of progress made, regardless of its magnitude.

2. Acknowledgments:

• A key element to success is cultivating gratitude. This involves appreciating the efforts, support of others and opportunities that contributed to the achievement of goals.

3. Reflection:

• Reflecting on the path to success is essential. This involves taking into account the challenges overcome, lessons learned and personal growth experienced along the way.

4. Celebration:

• Celebration is a tangible expression of success. Whether through personal reflection, sharing accomplishments with loved ones, or hosting a formal celebration, taking the time to rejoice in success reinforces its importance.

5. Positive self-talk:

• Accepting success means encouraging positive internal dialogue. This involves recognizing one's abilities, recognizing one's strengths, and reinforcing one's belief in one's ability to grow and achieve greater success.

6. Set new goals:

• Instead of relying solely on past accomplishments, accepting success often involves setting new goals. It reflects a forward-thinking attitude, encouraging a continuous cycle of growth and success.

7. Inspiration for others:

• Sharing your own success story can inspire and motivate others. Embracing success is not only a personal endeavor, but also an opportunity to positively influence and encourage those around you.

8. Balance humility and confidence:

• Accepting success requires a delicate balance between humility and confidence. It's about recognizing achievements with humility while maintaining confidence in your own abilities.

THE MEANING OF ACCEPT SUCCESS

1. Motivation and Confidence:

• Accepting success is a powerful motivator. Recognizing past achievements inspires confidence and provides a solid foundation for taking on new challenges and pursuing additional goals.

2. Positive Mindset:

• Cultivating a positive mindset is an important outcome for success. This involves focusing on the positive aspects of your journey, building confidence in your abilities and approaching future projects with optimism.

3. Resilience in the face of challenges:

• Accepting success contributes to resilience. People who have made it a habit to recognize and celebrate their achievements are often better equipped to meet challenges with a positive and determined attitude.

4. Satisfaction and personal development:

• Accepting success leads to a feeling of satisfaction and personal fulfillment. It asserts that efforts invested and goals pursued are aligned with personal values, contributing to a sense of purpose and satisfaction.

5. Develop a growth mindset:

• Success received with a spirit of growth becomes a springboard for further development. This reinforces the belief that skills can be developed through dedication and hard work, encouraging a continuous pursuit of improvement.

6. Cultivate a supportive environment:

• Celebrating success can help create a supportive environment. Sharing your accomplishments with friends, family, or colleagues fosters a culture of encouragement and shared success.

CHALLENGES TO ACHIEVE SUCCESS

1. Fear of complacency:

• Some people may worry that recognizing success will lead to complacency. However, embracing success is different from becoming complacent, as it involves maintaining a forward-thinking attitude and setting new goals.

2. External expectations:

• External expectations and social pressure can sometimes influence how success is perceived. Embracing success requires aligning personal definitions of success with internal values rather than conforming to external expectations.

3. Imposter syndrome:

• People who suffer from impostor syndrome may have difficulty accepting success, feel unworthy, or attribute their achievements to luck rather than personal abilities. Overcoming imposter syndrome is a crucial aspect of authentically embracing success.

Embracing success is a dynamic and continuous journey, rather than a destination. It involves a continuous cycle of setting and achieving goals, reflecting on achievements, and leveraging success as a catalyst for future growth. This mentality not only contributes to well-being and personal fulfillment, but also positively influences the environment, inspiring others to embark on their own path to success.

CELEBRATE THE STEPS

Celebrating milestones is a joyful and meaningful practice that involves recognizing and commemorating significant achievements, turning points and successes in life's journey. Whether big or small, milestones represent moments of achievement, growth, and perseverance.

IMPORTANCE OF CELEBRATING THE STEPS

1. Reflection and Gratitude:

• Celebrating milestones provides an opportunity for reflection and gratitude. This inspires people to look back on their journey, recognize the progress they have made, and express gratitude for the experiences and support that helped them get there.

2. Motivation and positive reinforcement:

• Recognizing and celebrating milestones is a powerful motivator. It provides positive reinforcement, builds confidence and encourages people to continue pursuing their goals and aspirations.

3. Sense of achievement:

• Milestones symbolize achievements, both personal and professional. Celebrating these moments creates a tangible and satisfying sense of achievement, validating the hard work and dedication put into achieving a goal.

4. Encourage a positive mindset:

• Celebrating milestones helps foster a positive mindset. It shifts the focus from challenges and obstacles to achievements and possibilities, generating optimism and resilience for future projects.

5. Develop self-esteem:

• Recognizing and celebrating milestones regularly contributes to the development of healthy self-esteem. This reinforces belief in one's own abilities and worth, creating a foundation for continued growth and success.

6. Create lasting memories:

• Celebrations associated with milestones create lasting memories. Whether through personal reflections, shared experiences with loved ones, or commemorations, these moments become an integral part of the life story.

WAYS TO CELEBRATE MILESTONES

1. Personal reflection:

• Take time for personal reflection to acknowledge the journey, challenges overcome, and lessons learned. Consider keeping a journal to document the thoughts and emotions associated with achieving each milestone.

2. **Express your gratitude:**

• Express gratitude to those who supported and contributed to the journey. Whether it's heartfelt messages, gestures of gratitude, or small tokens of appreciation, recognizing the role of others enhances the celebration experience.

3. **Set new goals:**

• The celebration of a milestone often marks a point of transition. Take this opportunity to set new goals and aspirations, creating a roadmap for the next phase of the journey.

4. **Community celebrations:**

• Share the joy with friends, family or colleagues during community celebrations. This could include gatherings, parties or shared activities that commemorate this milestone and strengthen social connections.

5. **Personal rewards:**

• Enjoy personal rewards to celebrate your achievements. This might mean doing a favorite activity, taking a meaningful trip, or acquiring a significant symbol.

6. Creative Commemoration:

• Adopt creative methods to commemorate milestones. This could include creating a visual representation, such as a vision board or scrapbook, to summarize the journey and achievements.

7. Recognize progress:

• Celebrate not only milestones, but also recognize small victories and incremental progress. Recognizing milestones reached along the way contributes to a continued sense of accomplishment.

8. Ceremonial acts:

• Consider incorporating ceremonies into the celebration. This could involve symbolic gestures, such as lighting a candle, planting a tree or creating a time capsule to mark the meaning of the moment.

OVERCOME CHALLENGES BY CELEBRATING STEPS

1. Downplaying Accomplishments:

• Some people may downplay their accomplishments and have difficulty celebrating milestones. Recognizing the value of personal achievements is essential to overcoming this challenge.

2. Comparisons with others:

• It is crucial to avoid comparisons with others. Every individual's journey is unique and milestones should be celebrated based on personal growth and aspirations rather than external criteria.

3. Fear of complacency:

• There is concern that celebrating milestones will lead to complacency. However, it is possible to celebrate achievements by maintaining a forward-looking attitude and setting new goals for continued growth.

In short, celebrating milestones is not just a momentary act; It is a holistic approach to embracing life's journey. These important markers serve as reminders of personal growth, resilience and the pursuit of aspirations. Whether through personal reflection, community celebrations or creative expression, recognizing milestones contributes to a positive and fulfilling life story. By celebrating achievements large and small, people cultivate a mindset of gratitude, motivation, and continued progress throughout their unique life journey.

GRATITUDE AND APPRECIATION

Gratitude and appreciation are powerful, transformative attitudes that involve recognizing and recognizing the value of people, experiences, and blessings in our lives. These feelings go beyond simple gratitude; They encompass a deep understanding of the positive impact that various elements contribute to our well-being. In this exploration, we delve deeper into the importance of cultivating gratitude and appreciation, their effects on mental and emotional well-being, and practical ways to integrate these attitudes into daily life.

THE MEANING OF GRATITUDE AND APPRECIATION

1. **Improved mental well-being:**

• Gratitude and appreciation have been linked to better mental health. By focusing on the positive aspects of life, people often experience reduced stress, increased happiness, and a greater sense of overall well-being.

2. **Positive relationships:**

• Expressing gratitude and appreciation strengthens relationships. Whether in a personal or professional context, recognizing the contributions of others promotes a positive and supportive environment, thereby improving the quality of connections.

3. Resilience in the face of adversity:

• Gratitude is a powerful tool for building resilience. In difficult times, people who practice gratitude are better equipped to find positives, learn from difficulties, and maintain a hopeful attitude.

4. Mindfulness and present life:

• Cultivating gratitude encourages mindfulness and present living. This encourages people to focus on the present moment, promoting awareness of the positive aspects of life that can often go unnoticed.

5. Emotional regulation:

• Regular expressions of gratitude contribute to emotional regulation. Recognizing positive experiences and relationships can counteract negative emotions, providing a more balanced and optimistic emotional state.

PRACTICAL WAYS TO CULTIVATE GRATITUDE AND APPRECIATION

1. Gratitude Journal:

• Keep a gratitude journal to periodically write down the things you are grateful for. This practice helps you focus on the positive aspects, no matter how small, thus promoting the habit of gratitude.

2. Express gratitude:

• Actively express your gratitude to others. Whether through verbal thanks, handwritten notes, or thoughtful gestures, recognizing the contributions of friends, family, and colleagues strengthens relationships.

3. Conscious reflection:

• Engage in mindful reflection, especially during difficult times. Identify lessons learned, personal growth or positive aspects even in difficult situations, promoting gratitude in adversity.

4. Gratitude rituals:

• Establish gratitude rituals in your daily routine. This could include taking a moment each morning or afternoon to reflect on the positive aspects of the day, creating the habit of appreciating life's blessings.

5. Volunteer and give back:

• Engage in acts of kindness and give back to the community. Volunteering not only benefits others, but also instills a feeling of gratitude for the ability to make a positive impact on the lives of others.

6. Savor the positive moments:

• Practice savoring the positive moments. Whether enjoying a beautiful sunset, enjoying a delicious meal, or savoring a moment of personal fulfillment, consciously enjoy these experiences.

7. Gratitude Challenges:

• Participate in gratitude challenges or initiatives. Some people find pleasure in participating in gratitude challenges on social media or in organized events that encourage the practice of gratitude.

8. Visual reminders:

• Use visual reminders to cultivate gratitude. This could include posting inspirational quotes, gratitude messages, or affirmations in visible locations as a daily reminder of the importance of appreciation.

OVERCOME CHALLENGES BY CULTIVATING GRATITUDE AND APPRECIATION

1. Cultural barriers:

• In some cultures, expressing gratitude is not a common practice. Overcoming cultural barriers involves recognizing the universal nature of gratitude and finding culturally appropriate ways to integrate it into daily life.

2. Overcome negative biases:

• The brain has a natural tendency to focus on negative experiences. Overcoming this negativity bias requires an intentional effort to redirect attention toward the positive through practices like keeping a gratitude journal.

3. Busy lifestyles:

• Busy schedules can make it difficult to prioritize gratitude. Incorporating small gratitude practices into daily routines, such as while commuting to work or before bed, can overcome the obstacles of a busy lifestyle.

In short, cultivating gratitude and appreciation is a transformative practice that contributes to a positive and fulfilling life. By actively recognizing the positives in our lives and expressing gratitude to others, we not only improve our mental and emotional well-being, but we also help create a more compassionate and supportive community. Gratitude is a skill that can be developed over time, and its practice creates a profound shift in perspective, allowing people to navigate life with a deeper sense of joy, resilience, and interconnectedness.

CHAPTER TWELVE

THE JOURNEY CONTINUES

"The journey continues" is a phrase that conveys the idea that life or a specific experience is an ongoing process and that there is much more to come. It suggests a feeling of progression, advancement, and continued personal growth or exploration.

This phrase is often used in a variety of contexts, including personal development, stories, and life events. This implies that, despite the challenges, achievements or milestones achieved, there is still much to experience, discover and achieve in the future. It can be a statement of optimism, resilience and a recognition that life is an ever-changing journey with ongoing opportunities for learning and growth.

"The Journey Continues" reminds us that each step, whether positive or challenging, contributes to a continuous and dynamic story. It encourages a forward-looking perspective, emphasizing anticipation of what awaits us on the personal, professional or life path.

MAINTAIN PROSPERITY

Maintaining prosperity involves a conscious and strategic effort to maintain and improve a state of long-term flourishing and abundance. It goes beyond momentary success or fleeting achievements and focuses on developing sustainable practices, mindsets and systems that support continued well-being and growth.

PRINCIPLES FOR MAINTAINING PROSPERITY

1. Holistic approach:

• Maintaining prosperity requires a holistic approach that encompasses multiple dimensions of life, including physical health, mental well-being, relationships, financial stability and personal fulfillment.

2. Adaptability:

• The ability to adapt to changing circumstances is essential to maintaining prosperity. Flexibility of mindset and strategies enable individuals to meet challenges, seize opportunities and remain resilient in the face of uncertainties.

3. Long-term vision:

• Developing a long-term vision is essential to maintaining prosperity. Setting clear, meaningful goals, both personally and professionally, provides a roadmap for continued growth and success.

4. Continuous Learning:

• A commitment to continuous learning and skills development is essential. Adopting a mindset of curiosity and pursuit of knowledge ensures adaptability in a rapidly changing world.

5. Financial Management:

• Maintaining prosperity requires responsible financial management. It involves budgeting, saving, investing wisely and making informed decisions to ensure a stable financial foundation for the future.

6. Resilience and coping mechanisms:

• Developing resilience and effective coping mechanisms are essential to maintaining prosperity. Developing the ability to recover from setbacks and cope with stress contributes to long-term well-being.

STRATEGIES TO MAINTAIN PROSPERITY

1. Goal Alignment:

• Ensure personal and professional goals align with values and contribute to overall well-being. This alignment fosters a sense of purpose, making the path to prosperity more sustainable.

2. Diversifications:

• Diversify experiences, skills and resources. This strategy mitigates risk and ensures that success is not overly dependent on a single aspect of life or a particular area of expertise.

3. Networking and Relationships:

• Cultivate and maintain a network of supportive relationships. Strong social connections contribute to emotional well-being and provide valuable support during difficult times.

4. Investment in health:

• Prioritize physical and mental health. Maintaining prosperity requires a foundation of well-being, and it is essential to invest in health through exercise, good nutrition, and mental health practices.

5. Adaptive leadership:

• In professional contexts, the adoption of adaptive leadership principles contributes to organizational sustainability. This involves anticipating change, fostering innovation, and guiding teams through constantly evolving challenges.

6. Strategic planning:

• Develop and execute strategic plans. Whether it is personal finance, professional development, or business operations, strategic planning ensures a proactive and intentional approach to maintaining prosperity.

TRANSFORMATIVE IMPACT OF MAINTAINING PROSPERITY

1. Constant well-being:

• Sustainable prosperity leads to constant well-being. People who actively cultivate various aspects of their lives experience a sense of fulfillment, satisfaction, and a lasting positive attitude.

2. Long-term achievements:

• The practices and principles associated with maintaining prosperity contribute to long-term flourishing. This is characterized by a deep satisfaction derived from a balanced and purposeful life.

3. Legacy building:

• Sustainable prosperity allows people to build a lasting legacy. This could be making positive contributions to the community, mentoring, or creating opportunities for future generations.

4. Positive impact on others:

• Those who maintain prosperity often have a positive impact on others. By sharing their knowledge, providing support and contributing to the well-being of the community, they create a ripple effect of prosperity.

5. Adaptability in the face of adversity:

• A state of lasting prosperity provides individuals with the adaptive capacity necessary to effectively confront adversity. Resilience becomes a natural response, ensuring that setbacks do not derail long-term success.

OVERCOME CHALLENGES TO MAINTAIN PROSPERITY

1. Complacency:

• Complacency can pose a challenge to maintaining prosperity. To overcome this problem, people must maintain a growth mindset, continually reevaluate their goals, and seek new challenges for continued development.

2. External pressures:

• External pressures, such as social expectations or economic fluctuations, can affect the maintenance of prosperity. Developing a resilient mindset and proactive strategies helps people resist external challenges.

3. Lack of adaptability:

• A rigid mindset or unwillingness to adapt can be detrimental to lasting prosperity. Cultivating adaptability involves embracing change, learning from experiences, and adjusting strategies accordingly.

In short, maintaining prosperity is a dynamic and continuous journey that requires intentional effort, adaptability, and a holistic approach to life. By aligning goals with values, investing in lifelong learning, and supporting various aspects of well-being, individuals can create the foundation for lasting success. Maintaining prosperity is not just about achieving a set of goals, but also about adopting a mindset and lifestyle that promotes long-term fulfillment, positive contributions to others, and a legacy that extends beyond individual achievements. .

INSPIRE OTHERS

Inspiring others is a powerful and inspiring endeavor that involves inspiring people to reach their full potential, pursue their goals, and overcome challenges with resilience. Whether in personal relationships, in leadership roles, or within communities, inspiring others creates a ripple effect of positivity and motivation.

PRINCIPLES TO INSPIRE OTHERS:

1. **Authenticity:**

• Authenticity is the cornerstone to inspiring others. Authentic, sincere actions, coupled with transparent communication, build trust and resonate with people, making inspiration more impactful.

2. Empathy:

• Understanding and empathizing with the experiences and challenges of others is essential. Compassion creates connection, allows people to feel seen and supported, thus fostering an environment conducive to inspiration.

3. Positive role model:

• Leading by example is a powerful way to inspire others. Demonstrating qualities such as resilience, dedication and a positive mindset sets a model that others can emulate in their own pursuits.

4. Effective Communication:

• Clear and effective communication is crucial. Expressing ideas, values and encouragement in a way that resonates with the audience ensures that the inspirational message is received and understood.

5. Recognition and encouragement:

• Recognizing the efforts and achievements of others is a fundamental principle. Providing genuine recognition and encouragement reinforces positive behaviors and motivates people to continue their journey.

STRATEGIES TO INSPIRE OTHERS

1. Active listening:

• Actively listening to others promotes a feeling of validation and respect. By understanding their views and concerns, you will be able to tailor your inspiration to meet their specific needs and aspirations.

2. Storytelling:

• Sharing personal stories of challenges, growth and success creates relatable narratives. The story creates an emotional connection, illustrating that it is possible to overcome obstacles and inspiring others to persevere.

3. Set high expectations:

• Setting high expectations communicates confidence in the abilities of others. It challenges them to step out of their comfort zone, thereby encouraging their personal and professional growth.

4. Provide mentoring:

• Providing mentoring and advice is a direct way to inspire others. Proposing ideas, sharing knowledge and offering support contribute to the development of those under your influence.

5. Encourage collaboration:

• Inspire a collaborative environment where people can learn from each other, share ideas and contribute collectively to common goals. Collaboration enhances creativity and fosters a sense of community.

6. Create a positive culture:

• Establishing a positive and inclusive organizational or social culture helps create an environment in which inspiration can thrive. A culture that values diversity, innovation and well-being promotes a sense of belonging and motivation.

TRANSFORMATIVE IMPACT BY INSPIRING OTHERS

1. Greater motivation:

• Inspiration increases motivation. People who are inspired by others feel a renewed sense of purpose and determination, which drives them to pursue their goals with enthusiasm and commitment.

2. Improved Performance:

• Inspired people tend to exhibit higher levels of performance. The belief that your efforts matter and contribute to a greater goal fosters a commitment to excellence.

3. Strengthened Relationships:

• Inspiration builds strong, positive relationships. Those who inspire others create a bond based on shared values, trust and a mutual commitment to growth and success.

4. Cultivation of leadership skills:

• Inspiring others is the hallmark of effective leadership. Those who inspire develop leadership skills such as empathy, communication and the ability to foster a collaborative and empowering environment.

5. Promotion of innovation:

• Inspirational leaders encourage innovative thinking. By fostering a culture that values creativity and forward-thinking, people are more likely to explore new ideas and approaches.

OVERCOME CHALLENGES BY INSPIRING OTHERS

1. Misalignment of Values:

• It is essential to ensure alignment between your values and those of the people you want to inspire. Misalignment can cause a lack of connection and hinder the effectiveness of inspiration.

2. Overcome resistance:

• Some people may resist inspiration due to personal obstacles or skepticism. Perseverance, patience, and an authentic approach can help overcome resistance over time.

3. Balance individual and collective inspiration:

• Balancing inspiration at an individual level while fostering a sense of collective inspiration requires a nuanced approach. It is essential to recognize and respond to the diverse needs within a group.

In short, inspiring others is a transformative act that allows people to reach new heights and realize their full potential. By embodying authenticity, practicing empathy, and using effective communication, you can create a positive impact on the lives of others. The ripple effect of inspiration extends beyond personal growth and influences communities, organizations, and societies. In the continuous journey of personal and collective development, the power to inspire becomes a catalyst for positive change and a legacy that resonates in the lives of those who grow.

CHAPTER THIRTEEN

CONCLUSION

In the final pages of "Break Free to Prosper: From Hardship to Success", we find ourselves at the intersection of reflection and anticipation, looking back on the transformative journey we have taken together. This book is more than a collection of words; has been a guide, a companion and a source of inspiration in breaking free from the shackles of hardship and embracing the limitless possibilities that success offers.

As you conclude this odyssey, remember that your journey does not end here: it evolves. The principles, strategies, and stories shared in these pages are not just static lessons but dynamic tools, ready to accompany you on the path to continued growth and prosperity. Echoes of resilience, triumphs over self-doubt, and unwavering pursuit of purpose are now woven into the fabric of her story.

You stand at the edge of your own narrative, equipped with the wisdom to identify limiting beliefs, the courage to overcome doubts, and the strength to face challenges. The importance of cultivating supportive relationships, fostering environments for growth, and distancing yourself from toxic influences has been ingrained in your journey. You've honed your resilience, defined your purpose, and set clear goals that align with the essence of who you are.

As you enter the realm of sustainable prosperity, remember that it is not just about achieving external indicators of success; it is about promoting holistic and sustainable well-being. You have learned the art of inspiring others, recognizing that true prosperity goes beyond personal triumphs to uplift those around you. His journey, with all its twists and turns, has become a beacon for those seeking their own path to prosperity.

In the next chapters of your life, continue to rely on inner strength, a prosperous mindset, and cultivating multiple streams of income. Embrace lifelong learning, develop your skills, and foster relationships that fuel your growth. Through the art of networking and leveraging connections, you will discover a vast reservoir of support and opportunities.

As you embark on the unwritten chapters, remember that defining your purpose is an ongoing journey. Setting clear goals becomes a compass that guides you through uncharted territories of personal and professional exploration. With a mindset shift toward prosperity, the power of positive affirmations, and financial empowerment, you will discover that you will not only exist, but thrive in every facet of life.

By adopting smart financial habits, creating multiple income streams and cultivating an entrepreneurial mindset, you will witness your potential unfold. The chapters that follow will demonstrate your commitment to lifelong learning, expanding your skills, and creating a support network that will propel you to success.

As you close the cover of this book, remember that your story does not end there; It evolves with every choice, every triumph, and every lesson learned. Embrace the unwritten pages with the same vigor that guided you through these chapters. Liberate yourself, flourish and let your journey inspire not only your own story, but also that of those who accompany you.

May the words contained within these pages guide you as you write the next chapters of your life, and may the journey ahead be a tapestry of prosperity, purpose, and unlimited success.

www.ingramcontent.com/pod-product-compliance
Lightning Source LLC
Chambersburg PA
CBHW071038290526
45795CB00004B/1211